W9-BPJ-870

Praise for
Mama's Got a Fake I.D.

"Caryn Rivadeneira is a real mom. With refreshing honesty, she casts vision and shares a perspective that every mom needs. If you've ever felt like you've lost yourself in the midst of raising a family, this book will help you find yourself again!"

> —JILL SAVAGE, mother of five; founder and CEO
> of Hearts at Home

"Caryn writes with humble and heartfelt authenticity, understanding the mixed emotions of motherhood. She unfolds a new and deep perspective for what it means to understand our real identity in Christ and why this is imperative to our lives as we navigate our passions and the potential to imprint our communities with God's hand."

> —DR. LIZ SELZER, director of leadership development
> and events for MOPS International and executive editor
> of *FullFill* magazine

"Finally, a book to shatter stereotypes that shackle moms! Caryn honors motherhood while challenging moms not to lose their unique personhood in this overwhelming stage of life. As a woman who has experienced this identity crisis myself, I'm grateful to Caryn for creating an insightful and much-needed book with the potential to empower moms to become all God designed them to be."

> —DR. SUE EDWARDS, assistant professor of Christian
> education at Dallas Theological Seminary

"I've met many moms who passionately love their kids, yet struggle with feeling marginalized. Does being a good mom *really* require them to surrender the goals and gifts that make them all God created them to be?

The good news is, it doesn't. With wit and wisdom, Caryn guides women who love being a mom through the process of rediscovering and reclaiming their full identity in Christ."

> —JANE JOHNSON STRUCK, executive editor of *MomSense* magazine; former executive editor of *Christian Parenting Today*

"While moms love their kids more than life itself, there is more to every mother than the title 'mom.' God wants mothers to live their fullest lives, and Caryn reminds us that in the throes of motherhood we can still continue to find our true identities in God."

> —TRACEY BIANCHI, coordinator of women's ministries at Christ Church of Oak Brook and speaker for MOPS International and other organizations

"I've heard mothers say that sacrificing their identity is part and parcel of being a good mom. Caryn shows us that the exact opposite is true. With humor and delightful insight, Caryn reveals that Jesus is thrilled to help every mom discover her unique identity. This is not a selfish side project but an essential way to worship God."

> —JONALYN GRACE FINCHER, apologist and author of *Ruby Slippers: How the Soul of a Woman Brings Her Home*

"Caryn has given us back those little pieces of ourselves we thought were gone for good. With a clear, biblical reminder that we are first and foremost the daughters of God, Caryn gently nudges us out from behind the false faces of maternal perfection and shows us how to reveal the women God created us to be, women of strength and vision and creativity and depth."

> —CARLA BARNHILL, author of *The Myth of the Perfect Mother* and former editor of *Christian Parenting Today*

"Caryn speaks for a lot of moms by openly discussing the difficulties of reducing a woman's identity to one label and a single season of her life. This book will be a refreshing read for moms who share that struggle. This book gives startling evidence that we need to reclaim God's richly multidimensional calling on his daughters' lives."

—CAROLYN CUSTIS JAMES, author of *The Gospel of Ruth*

"With a fresh mix of humor and understanding, Caryn speaks to the women I've heard from through the years: the women who feel invisible beyond their roles as moms. Caryn gives moms who struggle with their 'fake I.D.s' a voice and a way to find their true selves."

—GINGER KOLBABA, editor of *Today's Christian Woman* magazine

"This is a great read: humorous, straightforward, deeply theological, encouraging, and challenging. It will change the way you see yourself, other moms, and God himself. Once you start reading, you'll be changed and you'll discover new ways you can change the world."

—AMY SIMPSON, vice president of the Leadership Media Group of Christianity Today International and author of *Diving Deep: Experiencing Jesus Through Spiritual Disciplines*

"This is a conversation long overdue. Are there outside pressures to fit in? Yes. Is there just as much pressure in the faith world to fit in or conform? Sure. Thank goodness for an honest dialogue that takes women deeper as we celebrate the roles in our lives while exploring who God made us to be."

—T. SUZANNE ELLER, author of *The Woman I Am Becoming: Embracing the Chase for Identity, Faith, and Destiny*

"Caryn's fresh and practical perspective captured my attention—so much so that I let dinner burn as I tore through pages that reflected myself. This work is invaluable not just to mothers, but also to churches and families desiring to respect and appreciate moms for who we really are. I am grateful to Caryn for finally providing moms with such a soul-affirming resource."

—JULIE CLAWSON, author of *Everyday Justice*

"This delightful book is written for women like me. We are like Cinderella's stepsisters, who tried on the glass slipper of mommyhood and discovered a less-than-perfect fit. With humor, grace, and candid self-disclosure, Caryn encourages moms to embrace their God-inspired identity—never 'just a mom' but 'a mom and _____.' Find out how you might best fill in the blank."

—EILEEN BUTTON, columnist for *The Flint (Mich.) Journal*

"Did the picket-fence, 'I'm just a mom' role lose its paint in the fifties, and you've been waiting for someone—anyone—to point that out? Wait no longer. Caryn Rivadeneira and a whole new generation of Christian moms are trading paintbrushes for backhoes. Rebellious and deeply affirming, *Mama's Got a Fake I.D.* will help you explore the life-giving, Christ-empowering world after the picket fence comes down."

—SALLY MORGENTHALER, author of *The Emergent Manifesto of Hope*

Mama's Got a

FAKE I.D.

Mama's Got a FAKE I. D.

How to reveal the real you behind all that mom

Caryn Dahlstrand Rivadeneira

WaterBrook
PRESS

MAMA'S GOT A FAKE I.D.
PUBLISHED BY WATERBROOK PRESS
12265 Oracle Boulevard, Suite 200
Colorado Springs, Colorado 80921

All Scripture quotations, unless otherwise indicated, are taken from the Holy Bible, New International Version®. NIV®. Copyright © 1973, 1978, 1984 by International Bible Society. Used by permission of Zondervan Publishing House. All rights reserved. Scripture quotations marked (MSG) are taken from The Message. Copyright © by Eugene H. Peterson 1993, 1994, 1995, 1996, 2000, 2001, 2002. Used by permission of NavPress Publishing Group. All rights reserved. Scripture quotations marked (NKJV) are taken from the New King James Version®. Copyright © 1982 by Thomas Nelson Inc. Used by permission. All rights reserved.

Details in some anecdotes and stories have been changed to protect the identities of the persons involved.

ISBN 978-1-4000-7493-8
ISBN 978-0-30744-662-6 (electronic)

Copyright © 2009 by Caryn Dahlstrand Rivadeneira

All rights reserved. No part of this book may be reproduced or transmitted in any form or by any means, electronic or mechanical, including photocopying and recording, or by any information storage and retrieval system, without permission in writing from the publisher.

Published in the United States by WaterBrook Multnomah, an imprint of The Doubleday Publishing Group, a division of Random House Inc., New York.

WATERBROOK and its deer colophon are registered trademarks of Random House Inc.

Library of Congress Cataloging-in-Publication Data
Rivadeneira, Caryn Dahlstrand.
    Mama's got a fake I.D. : how to reveal the real you behind all that mom / Caryn Dahlstrand Rivadeneira.—1st ed.
        p. cm.
Includes bibliographical references.
    ISBN 978-1-4000-7493-8
  1. Mothers—Religious life. 2. Self-esteem/Religious aspects—Christianity. 3. Women—Religious aspects—Christianity. I. Title.
    BV4529.18.R58 2009
    248.8'431—dc22
                                        2008041569

Printed in the United States of America
2009—First Edition

10 9 8 7 6 5 4 3 2 1

SPECIAL SALES
Most WaterBrook Multnomah books are available in special quantity discounts when purchased in bulk by corporations, organizations, and special-interest groups. Custom imprinting or excerpting can also be done to fit special needs. For information, please e-mail SpecialMarkets@WaterBrookMultnomah.com or call 1-800-603-7051.

To Henrik, Greta, and Fredrik.
Mama loves you like absolute crazy.

Contents

Part 3: Get Out There and Be a Blessing

Acknowledgments

Like every aspiring author, I've been practicing these acknowledgments in my head since I was seven. Now that it's time to write them, of course, I'm drawing a complete blank. So let's just start with the man who, although he was a complete stranger, called me *mama*: thank you for lighting a fire in me to write *Mama's Got a Fake I.D.*

And thanks to Amy Simpson for telling me: "You should write a book about that." Thank you for your early encouragement and continued support. Which reminds me, thanks to Kevin Miller for all your kindness, help, and—along with Dave Goetz—for believing in the power and might of the at-home mom.

To all the members of my Big Mom Group: a Big Mom Thanks! While not all of you are quoted in these pages, each of you contributed to this book's shape in a big way. Thank you for your time, your stories, and your honesty. To all the other women who cheered me on—Sally Morgenthaler, Jonalyn Grace Fincher, Halee Gray Scott, Carla Barnhill, and Laura Polk (I know I'm forgetting a zillion more)—thank you heaps.

And Ron Lee, my editor: *muchas gracias.* Thank you for catching the vision, feeling my pain, and becoming a champion of not only this book but of all moms with fake I.D.'s. Thanks also to Pam Shoup and everyone else at WaterBrook Press who brought this book to life.

Thank you, Mom and Dad, for raising me to stay mindful of my gifts and with eyes open to God's possibilities. I love you both. And thanks to my in-laws—for all that baby-sitting and support. You are terrific.

As is my husband, Rafi: thank you, babe. I'm not the easiest wife in the world. Thanks for loving me anyway. I love you forever. And thank you, my best-ever kids, for your patience and love as I tried to milk every moment out of a day so I could do this "on the side." Thanks, too, for all the books and stories and drawings and everything else you made for me along the way. I thank God for you.

Which reminds me: thank you, God, for guiding this process and for throwing great people and great resources in my path. When people ask how I did this, I say (1) look at the disaster that is my house, and (2) look at the awesomeness that is my God.

Mama's Got a

FAKE I.D.

Hey, Wait!
That's Not Me

Go ahead and blame it on Dave. I do.

Were it not for Dave, I would never have had my first identity crisis as a mother. Had he not called and offered me a freelance job, which developed into an enjoyable—and highly fulfilling—opportunity to stretch myself, none of this would've happened.

Until my first son was six months old, I didn't realize I was losing my identity. Six months earlier I had left a dream job as managing editor of *Marriage Partnership* magazine to stay home with my new baby. I loved being home as Henrik's mom—still do. I remember spending what must've been days blowing raspberries on his toes to make him giggle and snuggling with him on the sofa just so I could watch his little mouth curl up into smiles and his lip pout out as he slept. (I confess, him napping on my stomach was a great excuse to catch up on long-past episodes of *Murder, She Wrote*—my very random favorite television show.)

I made up silly songs—which I still sing to him (to his horror) and to his siblings (to their delight). We strolled with our dogs through the neighborhood while I pointed out houses with porches that I liked. And we made faces at houses with additions that went all wrong. Those were great times.

Then my friend Dave called and ruined everything. He had started a business, and he needed an editor who could help him out. He suggested I work a few hours a week from home. It sounded cool (and exciting), so we met at Starbucks to work out the details. For ninety minutes we brainstormed and strategized. My head spun out ideas and possibilities. I hadn't done this sort of thing in six months, at least.

I loved it.

Things were going great—when the crisis hit. At the end of our meeting I stood up, closed my notebook (a spiral; this was pre-laptop), and shook Dave's hand. I hadn't felt this energized since before my son was born. And it wasn't just the creative energy that I was enjoying. It was something different, something completely unexpected.

I realized it had been months since I'd felt *this much like myself.* I couldn't help feeling a little guilty as I questioned why a brainstorming session over coffee was suddenly so compelling. This was not the way a new mom was supposed to feel. At least that's what I'd been led to believe.

A Closer Look at Myself

As I drove home, I kept asking myself what had just happened. As much as I loved spending days kissing my baby's toes, singing crazy songs, and taking walks, those things never gave me this kind of charge. And then I had to ask—the same questions you may be asking: *What kind of selfish person am I? Why doesn't motherhood give me this kind of rush? What does my excitement over a simple creative session say about who I am?*

Since these questions aren't the sort of thing a new mom readily admits to, I did what any reasonable mother would do: I kept them to myself. Besides, when I scooped Henrik up after I returned home, he greeted me rapturously with one of his trademark "Silence of the Lambs" open-mouth kiss/bites on the end of my nose. Suddenly, all monster-mother worries evaporated. I loved being a mom!

My boiling-over crisis settled to a quiet simmer.

Over the next couple of years I was blessed with another snuggly, giggly, wonderful baby (my Greta) as well as new, energizing projects with Dave's growing company. I continued to wrestle with the question of who I was, considering that what I did for most of the day (raise my kids) didn't charge me in the same way my freelance editing and writing did. Added to my identity crisis was a growing feeling of loneliness. No matter how much time I spent with other moms, none of them knew I felt like a freak of nature. I was a mom with two precious babies, and still all day I couldn't wait to get in my few hours of editing at night. How can you admit such a thing? Especially when all the other moms seem to thrive on nothing else but being moms.

Then I got another phone call. This time I was invited to become managing editor of *Christian Parenting Today* magazine (again, working part-time from home). In that new job my identity crisis eased a bit because I got to read letters and e-mail from readers. The amazing thing was that everyone else was *not* doing just fine, no matter how content my friends appeared to be.

The moms who contacted *Christian Parenting Today* struggled with the same issues of identity, feeling like they'd lost themselves and their abilities and dreams in the midst of motherhood. These moms—many of them around my age, with some younger and some older—were convinced that no one knew who they really were and, worse, that no one cared. They felt that others assumed too much, labeling them with the sanctioned Christian-mom profile and not bothering to get to know who they really were. Feeling too guilty, embarrassed, and alone to talk about this with their friends, they'd write to the magazine, revealing their secret shame. I felt the same way they did but had the advantage of reading all the letters.

I realized then that I wasn't a freak of nature. Many of us are in the same boat: The Moms Who Long to Be Known for Who We *Really* Are.

After that breakthrough, things really came to a head.

000

The winter before Henrik turned five, I was eight months pregnant with our third child. That might not sound like the ideal time to steal away for a weekend getaway, but my husband, Rafael, and I were invited to a retreat for "thoughtful" Christians. How could we resist a weekend in a rustic hotel on the snow-covered dunes of Lake Michigan?

We had a great time. It was relaxing and spiritually stimulating; we ate delicious food and enjoyed great company. It was all great except for one thing. An older man attending the retreat kept calling me *mama*. I can barely tolerate the maternity-ward nurse calling me mama—let alone a strange man! (And in case you're wondering: no, I did not let him touch my stomach.)

I can't fully describe how annoying this was, but as annoyed as I was with this man, I was actually more upset with myself for being so angry. While I oppose any language that stereotypes women or denies their full humanity, there was more going on here. After all, at eight months pregnant I was hugely, obviously a mama. So why couldn't I get over this?

Back in our room, I ranted about this man to Rafi. After he stopped laughing, he said, "You just hate being called a mom."

"I do not! I *love* being a mom."

"You love *being* a mom," he said. "But you hate being I.D.'d as one."

Ouch.

Rafi was right—mostly. I hated being labeled, but I love being known as a mom. The full truth is that I hated being identified *only* as a mom. When being a mom looms so large that it obscures everything else God made me to be, other people are not seeing the real me. They choose to disregard the truth that I'm Caryn and instead assume that I'm "career mom" or "preschool mom" or "smiling-and-waiting-for-the-school-bus mom." They seem to prefer a convenient label that supports their assumptions rather than going to the trouble of getting to know me. And as is the case with all stereotypes, that ain't me. It's a fake I.D.

Well, not entirely fake. In many ways I *am* a traditional at-home mom: I'm there when the kids wake up, take naps, eat lunch, watch cartoons, drink their chocolate milk. I carpool; I cook dinner; I play games on the floor; I bake like a champ. But those things don't give others the complete picture of who God made me to be. Same thing with any other mom. God gives important gifts to women that have nothing to do with conceiving, birthing (or adopting), and nurturing children. We have God-given talents, passions, and interests that a mom badge just doesn't bring to the fore. You need to dig below mom level to find this out. And when no one does, it gets lonely.

Sadly, the loneliest place for many moms is church. Ironic, isn't it? Especially since this is the place where we hope we'll be loved and accepted and encouraged to be the people God created us to be. But that's not the experience of most of the women I hear from. Listen to one woman's response to a blog titled "Why I Don't Do Women's Ministry":

> I never fit in with the women's groups…. It was always the same topics: kids, housework, crafts, and the other usual stuff. I would be sitting there wondering "Can't we talk about something else—like work issues and car repair…." In many churches they still try to push the June Cleaver prototype on women as the "biblical" model. And as a result, programs for women are "shallow, one-dimensional programs that miss important opportunities to minister to many women."[1]

Then there's my own story, as a woman who loved (and still loves) her church but struggled to find that fit, who even among friends felt misplaced at church. My fish-out-of-water feelings as a mom weren't affirmed or really talked about. And then there are the stories of women I know and those I've interviewed—the kind that would surprise you because the women seem to have it all together. They are sharp, funny, smart, engaging, articulate women. And that's not all: they seem to fit *so well* into church life (at least to me they seem to). But these women, too, have struggled with the same thing: they don't fit the mold, and they're not sure where they fit in the body of Christ.

Taking Responsibility—Finally!

At this point you may be nodding and even giving me a silent *Amen, sister!* But plenty of women (and a whole lot of men) are thinking, *Okay, blame your friend Dave and even the sexist "mama guy" at the retreat if you want. But* the church? *You've gone too far!*

Before I say any more about how lonely a mom can feel while sitting in church, I do realize there must be a few moms who have never wrestled with their sense of identity. This is not an easy thing to explore, because we tend to start wondering if we're simply turning into whiny, self-centered, disgruntled moms. With all the talk about identity, are we seeking to reveal our true selves or simply looking for sympathy? Wanting to be known for who we really are can seem so selfish, and what Christian woman wants that reputation?

None of us. But is it selfish to want to be known more fully? The creation account would lead us to believe otherwise.[2] I think something else is at work, and it is this: Christian women often earn an A-plus in self-condemnation while completely missing the class on honesty and transparency.

If you wish with all your heart that you could be known not just as a mom, but for *all* of who you are, let's find out who God made us to be. Let's learn how we can reintroduce ourselves to our families, our friends, our churches, and the world. Let's invite other people into our lives by telling them who we truly are.

Moms are a notoriously lonely lot,[3] and we are desperate to be *known* and loved for our entire selves. But because we are moms, we have limited time and opportunity to invest in becoming known, especially when we have to start by fighting our way out from behind assumption-packed labels. So while *at-home mom, soccer mom, work-at-home mom,* or *working mom* may be handy categories for the Bureau of the Census, market researchers, political strategists, and Bible-study planners, they hinder our ability to feel accepted, to be known, to belong, and to be used (in a good way) as the Body parts God intended! If we are to live and act as the women God created us to be, we need to chuck the labels and adopt new language that invites others to see us, know us, and turn to us as the women God made us to be.

It's Up to Us

There *is* a solution, and it gets back to those of us who are struggling with our identity. (I came face-to-face with this hard-truth solution in the midst of some serious self-pity, just so you know. Why can't God ever just allow us to wallow? Does he *always* have to interrupt us with wisdom and truth?) Okay, so now the solution: as easy as it is to blame "the church," we moms *are* the church! At least as much as anyone else. If the church is doing something wrong, then we are too (yes, I am blaming us now!). And if we want the church to change, it starts with us. It's up to us to change ourselves and the church. And we *can.*

I lost a lot of time blaming and hurting and hiding who I was and how I felt. That is, until I first wrote about the lost-identity issue for a blog I edit for Christianity Today International called Gifted for Leadership. I told about the stranger at the retreat who kept calling me *mama.* At the end, I opened up about what we moms can do about our crises. The response floored me—the positive comments as well as the not-so-nice ones! But the readers who wrote in and told their stories helped clarify what we need to do to help each other. It all starts with being open and telling people who we are.

God created us to bear his image in all of life, not just in one area.

I know that masses of women realize this, because they posted heartfelt comments on the blog, some that break your heart and others that make you want to cheer. (You'll hear from some of these women in later chapters, and you'll realize you are far from alone in your struggles.)

For many of us, the Bible teaching we've received and the church culture we operate in have shouted that we're *mothers* while just barely whispering that we are creations of God, crucial to the welfare of the church and of the world. Too often, those of us who wish others could see us as more than moms keep quiet about it, out of typical mom guilt and church-induced shame. As one woman posted on the blog: "Until we in the church can allow women to be honest about their identity crises without judging them as 'needing counseling' this problem will persist."[4]

So let's *do* something about this. We need to move this out from the shadows—the devil's true playground—and give it some light. Only then will we become known not for our mom roles but as complete women. We can set aside the broad categories and introduce ourselves to one another—and to the world—as the wonderful, talented, gifted women God created us to be. Only then can we live—and do—as God intended.

What's in Store

Well then, if you're a woman who loves being a mom but longs to be known, valued, and seen as a complete person, let's blow the lid off our secrets and change the world, starting with the church. By the end of this book, letting others know that you're a woman who is really worth knowing will be second nature. We'll toss our fake I.D.'s in the trash (let's recycle them, actually) and use new language to work up some legit credentials for the market researchers and those who organize women's events.

Since that weekend retreat, where I was nothing but *mama* to at least one stranger, I've spent a lot of time praying about, thinking about, talking about, reading about, and writing about this issue. I've learned life-changing lessons, which I'll share as honestly, practically, and thoughtfully as I can. And I've learned that I am far from alone in my questions and longings.

In the time we spend together, we'll go through the reasons why our identities matter to God, and why they should matter to others and to ourselves. We'll look at the cultural and church issues surrounding the identity crisis that moms face, as well as dig deep into the typical Christian response to all this.

By the end of this book, you'll have worked through your guilt, identified or reaffirmed your gifts (and better understood how they're to be used), and you'll have the confidence to flash your new I.D. to show others just who God created you to be. More importantly, you'll understand that your desire to be known has eternal significance. God can use your desire to be known and loved as a catalyst to inspire change in your church and community—and to make the church a place where all women are valued and embraced, encouraged and known.

At the end of each chapter, I've included questions for reflection and discussion. If you're using this book with friends, a reading group, a moms' group, book club, or any other group, even better! You can discuss the questions and take this journey together. If you're reading this book by yourself, join the discussion online on my blog at www.caryn rivadeneira.com. Through this, along with the stories from other moms, I hope you'll realize that this is a struggle most moms face. We're in it together, and it won't be a secret much longer.

CHAPTER 1

Being a Mom Makes You Much *More*

Here's an I.D. you can build on

Motherhood changes you. How's *that* for a bait and switch? But as much as I may be loathe to admit it when trying to stake out a fitting identity for myself and all us moms, having children shapes us in ways nothing else ever could. If the exhaustion, sickness, bulging belly, and peeing-while-sneezing of pregnancy or the anxiety-ridden, pressure-filled, stomach-tightening process of adoption doesn't key you in to this, simply driving for the first time with your child in the car will prove it. As soon as you become a mom, you're a changed woman.

My friend Carla Barnhill, who wrote one of the best books on motherhood ever, *The Myth of the Perfect Mother,* told me that when she became a mom, suddenly everyone else on the road became a maniac driver, fully devoted to ramming into her car. Of course, when she told me this, I was years away from having a child of my own, so I thought she was a complete psycho.

New Mom or Psycho?

I continued to think Carla was a psycho right up until the night my husband and I drove our precious new son, Henrik, home from the hospital.

I did fine all the way through two towns before we got to ours. *What a wuss, that Carla!* I thought. Then I had my husband stop at the friendly neighborhood grocery/drug store so he could run in and pick up some things to make my stitched-together nether regions feel better. And that's when I realized that I, too, was now a thoroughgoing psycho.

As soon as Rafi disappeared from view, I noticed he hadn't locked the driver-side door. And *the keys were in the ignition.* As I waited in the backseat with my new baby, panic struck. The people leaving the store, who just the week before would've looked like harmless, fun-loving teenagers, pleasant old men, kindly old ladies, key-jiggling dads, and parking-lot-scanning moms had morphed into gangs of carjackers casting a covetous look at a black SUV with a new mom and baby inside.

I felt completely helpless as I contemplated my predicament. I was trapped in the backseat by child-safety locks and the aforementioned stitches that prevented the sort of acrobatics needed to launch myself into the front seat. I wanted more than anything to swing my legs up and over and slide behind the wheel. Instead, I sat where I was with sweat pouring down my back. Even if I could have gotten behind the steering wheel, the strong post-delivery painkillers I had taken probably wouldn't have enhanced the driving abilities needed to flee that danger den. There was no way I could get my child to safety without agonizing pain, bloodletting, and probable jail time.

You should have heard me praying in the backseat. Desperate prayers of one big psycho mom were rushing up to God, pleading for protection against wanton teenage carjackers and suspicious-looking blue-haired ladies. I hadn't prayed that hard for anything since, well, two days earlier when I prayed, "Please, please, please Jesus, let this baby come *out!*"

God answered both of my prayers, of course. But I admit I'm still a bit psycho, and I figure as long as I have kids to care for and love, I'll be forever changed. I'm good with that, because these changes aren't for naught. Plus, the changes we undergo when we have children have *everything* to do with our identities. These changes shape us into the women God wants us to be.

Motherhood changes us in ways most of us never saw coming. (I could tell the story of me dunking my hand into a FULL toilet to recover a toy my daughter accidentally dropped during potty training, but I'll spare you.) Sure, being a mom is just one part of who we are. And being labeled as "Mom" and nothing else takes a woman created in God's image and reduces her to a role. But before we head into the reasons why we got mislabeled and some of the problems it causes, let's take a moment to celebrate some of the ways motherhood enhances who we are, makes us more fascinating (yes, *more*!), and fills out our identities in wonderful ways we couldn't have imagined.

Morphed by Motherhood

When I asked my "Big Mom Group" (the circle of women who shared stories for this book; the name is based on the group's size, not the women's!) how they'd been shaped and enriched by motherhood, they offered some terrific examples. What amazed me more than their stories, however, was how many of the themes overlapped. Let's look at some.

Your heart expands
No offense to our parents, siblings, spouses, pets, or any other loved ones, but honestly, until you had a child did you know you were capable of this kind of love?

Someone once told me that loving my child would fire up corners of my heart I didn't know were there. Was that ever the truth! Only a mom can know love that is this deep, penetrating, and desperate. This love makes us smile, laugh, cry, get angry, ache, and worry in ways we never knew we were capable of. This is the love that every woman in the Big Mom Group says is the best part of being a mom.

What's amazing about this love is that it's *beyond* feeling. It's more like having these things etched into our souls. Let me illustrate: A month or so before my older son was born, my mom asked me an odd question. "Caryn," she said, "you haven't ever felt unloved by me, have you?"

"No, of course not. Why?" I asked, bracing for some horrid words that would send me straight to the therapist's couch.

But instead she said, "Because it takes a bit. Don't feel bad if you don't feel that instant teary-eyed rush of love that some moms talk about. Just because you don't *feel* it yourself right away doesn't mean it's not there."

While I considered *her* a bit psycho for saying this, her words stayed with me. I became eternally grateful for them when I first held Henrik. While I was thrilled to have him in my arms, nursing away, and I knew immediately that I would machete anyone who tried to harm him, the "in love" feeling didn't immediately overwhelm me. But after we got home from the hospital there was the moment I'll never forget. Henrik stopped nursing momentarily and I looked down at him. Our eyes met in the darkness, he blinked, and I was a goner. That was it. The rush, the tears, my moment of complete love.

But, the psycho part of the love—the fear, protectiveness, and over-the-top readiness to take up arms to defend my child—came before the *rush.* I loved before I was in love. And I loved without having been loved first by my child. That's deep. That's a God kind of love, one that makes us more compassionate and understanding toward everyone.

I was reminded of this a few weeks ago when I got an e-mail from a friend. As I read the opening paragraph, I smiled from ear to ear. She had gotten pregnant—unexpectedly and very happily. But the tone changed as I read on. Early ultrasounds revealed a problem with the pregnancy. She was told to prepare to miscarry. I was crying as she concluded her e-mail by sharing the story of her miscarriage and adding a call for prayer.

While my friend's e-mail under any circumstances would have made me feel bad, before I had kids, I wouldn't have cried after reading it. My heart just didn't work that way back then. I was more black and white, practical. Honestly, I remember hearing of other people's miscarriages and thinking, *God knows what he's doing.* While God does know what he's doing, I will never again be so unaffected by another mother's loss.

Your eyes open

My next-door neighbor Kathryn told me one of her favorite things about being a mom is that now she sees the world differently. "With kids," she says, "parades, the zoo, Disney World, everything looks so different!"

How about it. For me, what used to be a regular walk through the neighborhood or down by the creek has, with kids, become an adventure, a time to discover, giggle, and goof off. I see things I never noticed before and pay attention to things I used to think didn't matter.

But it's not just in these physical sorts of things that our eyes are opened. We see the *state* of the world around us differently. Sort of a mom's-eye view of the world. Suddenly, we see so clearly the agony of a broken world—a woman too poor and hungry to nourish her baby, the hurt of the unloved or orphaned child. And it's hard *not* to react.

Shayne Moore, a blogger for GiftedForLeadership.com, felt this tug that led her to get involved with Bono's ONE Campaign. "Being a mom certainly pressed me toward being socially minded and wanting to leave a better world to my children," she writes. "And when it comes to the AIDS crisis, I couldn't see myself turning my back and in twenty years have my kids ask me about it and the only response I would have was, 'Oh, yeah. I think I remember hearing something about that…'"[1]

So she did something. "The words of Scripture, 'Be a voice for the voiceless,' started to be a silent rhythm in my steps. In 2005 I traveled to Kenya with my church. While in Kenya I visited an HIV/AIDS clinic, and I watched as a woman left with some lifesaving medication in her hands. Her small son trailed behind. I turned to the nurse next to me and asked where the medication came from. As the nurse told me, I realized the ARVs [antiretrovirals] came from the funding I, along with other Americans, had lobbied President Bush and Congress to support.

"I still smile as I think about that Kenyan mother. It's true that some extraordinary things have happened through my involvement with the ONE Campaign, but mostly I'm that ordinary stay-at-home mom who's now a voice for the voiceless."[2]

Your perspective and priorities change

This is the one we all talk about—the move from self-centered to sacrifice, sacrifice, sacrifice. Right? No one likes to admit she was once self-centered. Even though I totally *was* self-centered in the worst way, I won't assume that about you. What I mean by "self-centered" is that the decisions of life were ours to make. Where we went to school, what job we pursued, the food we ate, the television programs we watched, where we went on vacation. Those life decisions were up to us (and our spouses, if applicable). This is not to say we were never considerate of others or mindful of the effects of our decisions, but you know what I'm talking about.

Then you have a child and your life is no longer your own. The sacrifice of motherhood shows up in a million ways. For some it means trading the city they love for a bland suburb where houses come with great backyards. For others it means trading jobs they love for ones that allow more time with their kids. For still others it means that weekly dance class gets pushed off or that garden doesn't look as good as it once did. We've all given up at least one important thing so we can invest in our kids, and we've done it gladly—out of that psycho love.

Author and friend Carla Barnhill writes that her favorite part of being a mom was "watching another person become."[3] She's right, huh? When your day's agenda includes learning about and enjoying the people your children are becoming, it makes sacrificing easy and rewarding—to a point, that is.

You find an outlet for something you do exceedingly well

A few years ago, my friend Ruth had a baby with Down syndrome. When I stopped her father-in-law at church to ask how Ruth and her new son were doing after he had some minor surgery, her father-in-law said: "You know, we knew Ruth was a great mom before. But wow, the way she's dealing with all that has come at her is showing her true colors. And they're beautiful."

He was dead on. The challenges of mothering bring to the forefront skills, abilities, and strengths we had all along but hadn't yet had an opportunity to use. And it's not just the "mothering" gifts that get sharper, of course. Stephanie says, "I'm so much more well rounded since becoming a mom!" And who isn't? Think of all the stuff you've got to get good at in a hurry—things like first aid, nutrition, repairing broken things, storytelling, coaching, cheering. Go ahead, add to the list.

Writer and Big Mom Group member Valerie Weaver-Zercher says, "Motherhood has intensified my desire to write and has become much of what I write about these days. In that way, it's been my greatest Muse ever, and I'm grateful for that."

That gets a big ditto from me, by the way! Even if you're not a writer, musician, or artist, just think how your creativity is ignited by motherhood. I was never much of a songwriter before kids (okay, so I made up a *couple* of tunes for my dogs), but my kids are familiar with all sorts of silly songs I've composed just for them.

Because we have set other things aside for now, our gifts—the things we love and do well—become more important than ever. The mother of one of my son's friends once played tennis competitively for a Big Ten school. Recently, she told me that she got back into competitive tennis because it was either that or "therapy." She was laughing when she said it, and I'm happy to report that she's better than ever—as a mom *and* tennis player.

You get to join the in-group

This is where things almost get spooky: Once you're a mom, you understand things in whole new ways, and you connect with other moms in new ways. The spooky part is that it's something like having your own language. Years ago, I wrote about a secret ministry that existed in my church's narthex: the club of moms (and dads actually) who gather outside the sanctuary with their crying—and not-quite-ready-for-nursery—babies. While I've never been good at rolling out the welcome wagon at church (not a gift), when I'm out there with my baby and notice a new parent with a baby in arms, it's second nature to go up to chat and get that wagon rolling.

There are things you don't understand until you're a mother. My neighbor Kathryn calls this the "kinship" of motherhood. That's a great word. As different as we are, when we become moms we join a sort of maternity fraternity (sort of—but the rhyme is fun).

As a shy person who always feels awkward starting conversations with new people, I love that having kids always provides fodder for conversation. (The trouble comes when it becomes the *only* fodder for conversation!) And I love that motherhood connects us in a, well, familial way. I used to think this same thing when I'd see smokers congregated outside a building. Since I'm not a smoker, this will sound weird. But I used to look at them and think, *Must be nice to have something you all have in common right off the bat.* Motherhood's like that. Except that motherhood actually can *extend* your life.

But I digress. A little while back I got a call from the younger sister of one of my childhood best friends. She had a new baby who refused to sleep. To know me is to know I've had three babies—who wouldn't sleep. I'm kind of the woman moms of sleepless babies call to commiserate with. So Suzy called, wanting to know if I had discovered any tricks of the trade or knew of any good books. (While I have not discovered any tricks, I am a fan of Dr. Marc Weissbluth's *Healthy Sleep Habits, Happy Child.* You can read Henrik's story on page 127!) But at the heart of the call was Suzy's desire to hear from another mom who'd been there. To hear that she was doing okay. That she wasn't a bad mom for not knowing how to get her child to sleep. She wanted the reassurance that it would get better, that her child would one day sleep, that one day *she* would sleep. And that in the end, it would all be okay.

That's the sort of thing another mom can deliver best. That's why we need one another and why the transformation into "one of the moms" is such a blessing.

Your faith gets a boost

Just before Christmas 2007, after getting a chill as I read Luke 2:34–35, I posted this on my blog:

> I think feeling this [chill] deepened my understanding of the entire story of God's redeeming love for us. From what it really meant and entailed for God to send his Son to save us to what it meant for Mary to bear and raise her boy, the Messiah, to what it means for me as a mother to raise my own boys and girl to grow to love and know that same Messiah.
>
> While perhaps I was just dense in my reading of this passage before (and surely you don't have to be a mom to catch the significance), this isn't the only passage or instance I've noticed where my being a mom heightens my understanding of Scripture along with my understanding of (and questions for!) God.
>
> While I expected motherhood to change me in many ways, getting to know God better by being a mom surprised me.[4]

I could go on and on about the ways watching my children grow, learn, and play has given me insight into the heart of God and taught me lessons, but instead I'll share one I got from a woman who commented on this very post.

Being a mother taught me one of my most important lessons. After a particularly difficult morning with my seven-year-old daughter, I sat on the love seat, holding her while we both cried. She had been crying and demanding that she didn't want to go to school. I had insisted that she would go. While I drove her to school, she complained the whole way. As we walked to her schoolroom, she loudly resisted the whole way. Her teacher, hearing the commotion, suggested that I let her stay home for the day.

As I held her while we cried, I lamented that she didn't like school. I had loved school, loved reading and learning. I thought about all she would miss if she wasn't a reader. As I cried with her and prayed, I realized that I was wanting my daughter to be more like me. I had to surrender that right to God and ask him to forgive me for expecting her to be like me instead of who she was. When I did, I realized that I needed to accept her just the way she was—the way God had made her, not a carbon copy of me. I realized that I really did love her just the way she was— uniquely Reese.

It was then that the truth that God loves me just the way I am made its journey from my head to my heart. In accepting my daughter just as she was, I received God's unconditional acceptance and love for myself. My tears were no longer tears of disappointment or frustration but pure joy.[5]

Getting to the Point

Obviously this just scratches the surface of the changes we moms experience. We all know about the physical changes, the physiological changes (hormonal issues, depression, etc.), and the ways motherhood can actually make us *worse* people. (Before I had kids, I'm pretty sure I could get through the day without yelling at *somebody*!) But these changes are part of the wonder of being a mom—along with the joy of getting to love, nurture, and cheer on the best kids ever.

But what *exactly* am I getting at here? It's more important than we realize to understand the changes we experience. Because by acknowledging the ways we change, we also acknowledge the ways we don't. And as all-encompassing as the changes might seem, no matter how different you feel, *you*—the woman God made you to be—are still very much you.

In fact, now that I've been tossing around the word *change*, I'd actually like to offer up a more accurate term. Look at yourself a minute; look at who you really are: motherhood doesn't *change* you as much as it *refines* you.

My neighbor Kathryn says, "Being a mom stretches, shapes, and molds you." I like that too. Because when you're refined, stretched, shaped, or molded, the core doesn't change. The essential elements stay the same. It's true that the transformation is overwhelming because our perspectives, focus, and priorities change. It can seem that we've experienced a complete metamorphosis, leading us to feel like we've lost ourselves. Hence our identity crises and the sense of loneliness and isolation.

In reality, the changes of motherhood don't make us *less* of who we are—but *more*. God refines us to make us more of who he wants us to be.

The transformative process of motherhood is not unlike that of becoming a Christian. (If you're not one, I hope you can experience this someday!) The Bible is filled with language referring to God's refining his people as helping them "become" (in the word of my friend Carla). Malachi 3:2 says, "Who can endure the day of his coming? Who can stand when he appears? For he will be like a refiner's fire or a launderer's soap." Psalm 66:10 says, "You, O God, tested us; you refined us like silver."

In the next two verses we read how God's people were refined: "You brought us into prison and laid burdens on our backs. You let men ride over our heads; we went through fire and water, but you brought us to a place of abundance."

Now on a good day motherhood sounds nothing like this. But on a normal-to-bad one…? Maybe not so much the fire and water, but feeling trapped, burdened, ridden on (literally) all sound like the hard work of raising kids. Most of the time, these refining experiences leave us feeling beat down and lost. But remember, this passage describes *refinement* and ends up in a place of abundance. That means more—not less.

The changes of motherhood make us more unique, more ourselves, more capable, more self-sacrificing, more loving, more confident, more understanding of God, more discerning, and more of the women God made us to be.

So how did everyone get so confused, thinking that motherhood stripped us of who we really are? How did we get mislabeled? After you stop and reflect on the questions for this chapter, let's take a look at where it all went wrong—and how we can get it to be all right.

QUESTIONS FOR REFLECTION AND DISCUSSION

- Can you think of anything in life that has changed you as much as motherhood? If so, what is it?
- How has motherhood changed you the most—in both good ways and otherwise?
- How are you "more of who God made you to be" as a result of being a mom? (Think in terms of being more resourceful, confident, courageous, creative, compassionate, competent, and selfless.)
- Do you benefit from being in the "maternity fraternity"? If so, how has being one of the moms affected your life?
- In what ways has motherhood given you new insights into God's character?

PART 1

How Moms Keep Losing Their I.D.'s

(and why we need them back!)

CHAPTER 2

How Designer Women Got a Generic Label

"Mom" might be easy to remember,
but one size does not fit all

Last summer, Rafi and I spent an evening with a group of my friends and their husbands on a beautiful sailboat. (It belongs to one of us; unfortunately that one is not me.) We sailed on Lake Michigan, enjoying the Chicago skyline, munching on sandwiches, telling stories, laughing about our crazy lives. As I enjoyed a wonderful evening with this motley crew of friends, I couldn't help but think about all the ways moms get mislabeled.

On paper, each of the four women was the same. (Imagine a list on a market researcher's desk or a member log at a women's ministry planning meeting.) Each woman is a middle-class, middle-American, college-educated, married, Christian, thirty-something, at-home mom. Sheesh. We were even all blond! Sitting in the back (or *aft*, for all you sailors) of that boat were four perfectly packaged Christian moms. Trouble was, of course, those packages said nothing about us as individuals. Despite the demographic similarities, we could not be more different.

For example, while we all fall into the "at home with our kids" category, that says nothing about our approaches to or philosophies of motherhood. It doesn't even say anything about what our days or lives look like.

There was Betty: a tireless activist and the mother of four boys. She is also an educator and a fund-raiser for researching a cure for the Type I diabetes that afflicts her oldest son and breaks her heart.

There was Kathy: mother of two boys and a girl, part-time hairdresser, and the most well-connected woman I know. She's the most natural—dare I say "normal"—evangelist too.

There was Shawna: mother of one girl. A painter and adventurer who climbed Mount Kilimanjaro last summer (wearing a T-shirt that raised awareness for Betty's diabetes campaign). As a result of her world travels, Shawna now invests her passion and talent in raising awareness of the plight of some of the world's neediest people.

Then there was me: you've heard enough about me—and we're only two chapters in—so I'll stop here.

My three friends and I differ on so many other things—what we feed and buy for our kids (and ourselves), the schools we choose, where we worship, for whom we vote, and what we envision for our own futures. We're great friends; we talk and laugh easily. Our differences bond us and add enjoyment to our time together. But as different as we are, we still get crammed into the same box and slapped with the same label. We are complex and multifaceted women, complete persons created by God. But each of us has gotten lost in motherhood.

In case you're wondering, by the way, it's not just at-home moms who feel this way. My friend Anne (a career woman who's married to an at-home dad) says that even with the "working mom" label, people seem to focus only on the mom part, not the working part. "It really doesn't matter what I do—the focus is still the kids," she says. "People assume I only work because I have to, not because I actually enjoy it and am good at it."

Then there's the darker side of generic labeling. "I think the label 'working mom' sort of suggests that my kids aren't that important to me, or at least they're not my top priority," says Amy, a publishing executive and the mother of two girls. "It also suggests that I've sacrificed them at the altar of my career or I really want to be a man or something."

Amy knows whereof I speak. Although she has been crammed into a different box from the one I've been in and perhaps a different one from your experience, isn't she basically describing your experience and mine—as moms who have been given a false label?

So how did women who have so much to offer not only their families but the world end up with these fake I.D.'s?

Where It All Went Wrong

In chapter 1 we looked at the wonderful ways we change when we have children. And frankly, once we understand the ways we've changed, it's *sort of* easy to understand how we got mislabeled and misunderstood and why we get lumped together as if there is only one standard-issue mom role on the entire planet. You can *kind of* figure out how some people get confused, thinking, *Well, they all change. They must change into the SAME THING!*

At least from the outside looking in, it's easy to understand why people might assume we all morphed into the everymom, fresh off the assembly line. People assume that because motherhood has such power to sharpen us, shape us, and sort of refurbish us, it has the power to make us all the same person.

Case in point: when was the last time you told someone you were a mom and heard back, "Fascinating! Tell me about yourself!"? Doesn't happen, right? (If it does, call me. I want to run in your circles!) Instead, you'll get asked about your kids—about whom you'll gladly gush—and the conversation will drift away from what you're all about. Come on now—we all either have moms, know moms, or are moms. So who needs to ask more, right?

And yet there was a time when moms were considered *interesting* in their own right. Take a look at the ever-popular Proverbs 31 woman:

The "Wife of Noble Character" whom I will temporarily rename the "Mom of Noble Character."

Here's our Noble Mom as described in Proverbs 31:10–31:

A wife of noble character who can find?
    She is worth far more than rubies.
Her husband has full confidence in her
    and lacks nothing of value.
She brings him good, not harm,
    all the days of her life.
She selects wool and flax
    and works with eager hands.
She is like the merchant ships,
    bringing her food from afar.
She gets up while it is still dark;
    she provides food for her family
    and portions for her servant girls.
She considers a field and buys it;
    out of her earnings she plants a vineyard.
She sets about her work vigorously;
    her arms are strong for her tasks.
She sees that her trading is profitable,
    and her lamp does not go out at night.
In her hand she holds the distaff
    and grasps the spindle with her fingers.
She opens her arms to the poor
    and extends her hands to the needy.
When it snows, she has no fear for her household;
    for all of them are clothed in scarlet.
She makes coverings for her bed;
    she is clothed in fine linen and purple.

Her husband is respected at the city gate,
>   where he takes his seat among the elders of the land.

She makes linen garments and sells them,
>   and supplies the merchants with sashes.

She is clothed with strength and dignity;
>   she can laugh at the days to come.

She speaks with wisdom,
>   and faithful instruction is on her tongue.

She watches over the affairs of her household
>   and does not eat the bread of idleness.

Her children arise and call her blessed;
>   her husband also, and he praises her:

"Many women do noble things,
>   but you surpass them all."

Charm is deceptive, and beauty is fleeting;
>   but a woman who fears the LORD is to be praised.

Give her the reward she has earned,
>   and let her works bring her praise at the city gate.

I understand that you get a bit sick of this overachiever as your model for Christian womanhood, but look more closely. Say what you want about her—but this woman has *depth*. She is not just accomplished beyond any normal measure of human accomplishment; she's *interesting*. I daresay someone would meet this Mom of Noble Character at a party and say, "Fascinating! Tell me more!" And while you can tell from reading portions of the Bible that women weren't usually held in the highest of esteem, this passage shows that "noble" women had a *lot* more than their mom roles going on. Leave it to God to look this deeply into a woman's identity and give us a glimpse of her talent, intelligence, creativity, and impact on the world.

My favorite part of this whole thing? If you go back to the first verse of the chapter, you'll see where King Lemuel learned all this wisdom: from his mother. She's *interesting,* and she didn't try to hide her abilities and accomplishments—least of all from her son.

Somewhere between our Noble Mom of the ancient past and moms of today, when it comes to the way we view moms, we got way off track. I won't try to review the woes of mothers (and women in general) throughout history. It's more helpful for our purposes to take a quick look back at recent history to understand how moms got mislabeled.

False Labels in Recent History

Not long ago Halee Gray Scott—a professor friend—e-mailed me this quote from Margaret Mitchell's *Gone with the Wind.* (I got her hooked on Harry Potter; she's trying to get me hooked on Russian lit and *Gone with the Wind.*):

> It had begun to dawn on him that this same little pretty head
> was a 'good head for figures.' In fact, a much better one than
> his own and the knowledge was disquieting.... He thought
> [business] all beyond her mental grasp and it had been pleasant
> to explain things to her. Now he saw that she understood
> entirely too well and he felt the usual masculine indignation
> at the duplicity of women. Added to it was the usual masculine
> disillusionment in discovering that a woman has a brain.[1]

Halee ended her e-mail with: "I laughed out loud for a long time at this one!"

Me too! Except I didn't find it so unbelievable. Halee doesn't have kids (at least not as I write this), so she doesn't know that even with a Ph.D., if and when she does have kids, she'll run into someone who'll be surprised she's got a brain.

For moms, the passage from *Gone with the Wind* isn't so funny, simply because this sort of thinking *still exists*. Mitchell wrote her epic novel in 1936—and she was describing the world of the Civil War and Reconstruction, about seventy years prior. While we've certainly come a long way, baby, some attitudes die hard.

I'm of the blessed generation (I was born in 1972) of women who grew up thinking we could do or be anything. I was never taught that there are things only men are capable of doing. Throughout my schooling and career, I haven't encountered anyone who outwardly indicated that my gender might affect my mind or my gifts. But while I escaped gender-related bias in my career, I know women who regularly get labeled with the mindless-mom stereotype. When you start sniffing around recent history, you get a whiff of the fuel that fed that stereotype.

In her essay "The Human-Not-Quite-Human," Dorothy L. Sayers suggests the Industrial Revolution robbed women of their *meaningful* work in life. As more and more of the industries that were dominated by and excelled in by women—"spinning, weaving, baking, brewing, distilling, perfumery, preserving, pickling"[2] to name a few—were removed from a woman's life via technology and relegated to the world of men and business, a woman's world became, frankly, blander, as she returned "to the home from which all intelligent occupation has been steadily removed."[3] According to Sayers, in its attempt to bring us more leisure, the Industrial Revolution robbed women of the meaning and "intelligence" that once were givens in their domestic tasks and responsibilities.

I can sense many of you getting jittery, even defensive. And I don't blame you. Remember, I'm typing this as one of my kids sleeps and the others are outside playing. When they come back inside, I will stop writing and return to my primary role as their mom. I don't think that all things domestic lack meaning—or even intelligence. The things I do with my children have eternal meaning. No matter what else we do in life, we will be most proud of the job of raising and loving our children.

Many—if not most—of us relish every opportunity to get down and dirty with our maternal gifts. However, those of us who are not abundantly *gifted* in the neotraditional domestic duties risk stagnation if we don't realize that the devaluing of motherhood and the essential contributions of women are *recent* developments. The truth is that the neotraditional gifts associated with motherhood do constitute "intelligent occupation" for many women (e.g., those of you who got jittery and defensive a minute ago) because they get to live out their gifts, dreams, and talents by raising their children. And that's awesome! But for other women, domestic tasks are less fulfilling because God didn't equip them in the same way.

When industrialization stripped women of more "productive" work (read: work that generated an income), society closed off outlets in which women who were gifted in a variety of ways could live and shine and be valued as God made them. When American culture limited women, it was assumed that women actually desired a simpler and less-varied life. Eventually, it was assumed that women were not capable of great accomplishments beyond the nurture of children.

The blame doesn't end with the Industrial Revolution. The thinking that if a woman is "at home" she must have nothing else going on got a big boost during the 1950s and 1960s. My friend Carla thinks television's *The Adventures of Ozzie and Harriet* and *Leave It to Beaver* in those decades helped indoctrinate a generation. She writes:

> The 1950s are the epitome of all that is good and holy in family life—Dad at work, Mom at home, the three-bedroom house with a yard, a dog, a station wagon, and two happy, smiling children. This is the family we are trying to live up to....
>
> We have translated the '50s model of the perfect American family to the model of the perfect Christian family. In doing so, we have taken away a woman's ability to follow God's leading in

her life and replaced it with a kind of bondage to an ideal that isn't consistent with the call of Scripture.[4]

I think she's dead on. Even *I* idealize the Ozzie-and-Harriet world. Vacuuming in heels and one of those cool, tight-fitting sweater sets, with plenty of crinoline under my skirt and pearls around my neck? Yes! Passing my time gossiping with the neighbor lady while sipping coffee until it's time to get my husband's after-work drink and paper ready? It's so uncomplicated. Who wouldn't be drawn to motherhood that is so undemanding?

While I'm grateful that worlds have opened up to moms since the 1950s, part of me does long for the order, the structure of the idealized world of Harriet Nelson and June Cleaver. After all, the TV moms from back then look so unruffled. If only it were true.

In the end, I much prefer reality to television's fantasy world. We honor God when we honor his creation—women in all their roles, using all the gifts God gave them. When we assign fake I.D.'s to moms, we not only fail them, we fail God.

Your Fake I.D. and Mine

False I.D.'s for moms are plentiful, so take your pick: *at-home mom, working mom, work-at-home mom, soccer mom, alpha mom, hybrid mom, momprenuer* (though I have to admit, I really like these last two—I mean *how intriguing* are they?). *You* know you're not a label, but market researchers still haven't caught on.

Like most falsehoods, there is a thread of truth in these labels. For instance, the needs of a working mom will differ drastically from those of an at-home mom (say, for example, an evening out sounds great to the at-home mom, while not so much for the working mom). But the one-dimensional categories created by marketers are the least of our worries.

The fake I.D.'s I worry about are the "cultural expectation" labels, the labels you get stuck with from the environment in which you operate. We could call this your community I.D., meaning: how do those you are around the most view you? What assumptions do they make? This is where things turn fake fast.

In her book *Ruby Slippers: How the Soul of a Woman Brings Her Home,* Jonalyn Grace Fincher calls these cultural assumptions our "corsets." (Wish I would've thought of this.) In describing the corset of a good Christian mother, for instance, Jonalyn writes:

> I live for my children, drive for my children, shop for and read
> to my children. Get the minivan, filter out all the "bad" stuff in
> their lives, be it sugar cereal, Harry Potter, or contact sports. I
> make a hot supper every evening. But what if I hate cooking?
> Or what if I want to finish college or go to law school? What if
> I don't really like being with kids all day long? What if I want
> to work on something other than long division and laundry?
> Can I be both a mom and a woman with other interests?[5]

I'm a woman who runs in Christian cultural circles, and I'd say this expectation sounds about right. These are the areas in which I start feeling the squeeze when I don't "match up." And since, let's see, I don't drive a minivan, my kids eat sugar cereal (often with me!), I *read them* Harry Potter and don't have huge contact-sports issues, I'm busting out of my corset (though not in the good way—except when I'm nursing). I don't even call the evening meal *supper!* I call it *dinner.* However, I do prepare it, every night, and I do like to cook. And I actually try to cook with love because I think it makes the food taste better. (There, the corset's feeling better already…)

But seriously, Jonalyn raises excellent questions. What *does* happen when and if we want to be *more* than these assumptions allow? What happens when your community I.D. is all wrong for you and you fail to live up to anyone's expectations? What do you do when, since you don't "fit," no one wants to get to know you?

Frankly? Things get dark.

Read a mom-oriented magazine or watch *Oprah*,[6] and you'll hear it: again and again moms rate loneliness and loss of self as two of their biggest issues. And these are *big* issues! Of course, loneliness often has to do with the *physical* separation from others that the at-home crowd can feel most acutely, but I think this can have more to do with the *emotional* separation—or perceived separation—that occurs when we don't fit in. Truth is, no matter how often you're around other people—even other moms—if you feel like you aren't understood, appreciated, valued, or known (or worth knowing) as the real you, you're alone.

In fact, when I asked my Big Mom Group to name the setting in which they struggle most to be known and to fit in as their real selves, the number-one answer was *with other moms!* (Church followed at a close second. You can read more about this in chapter 5.)

One mom (I'm going to keep these answers anonymous—I'd hate to isolate anyone further!) told me she struggled most with the "good, holy, rich, have-it-together moms." While she admitted this characterization was probably more in her mind than a demographic reality, "they do such a good job of making it seem real. I feel nearly invisible, like a background mom among them."

Another mom said, "Some Christian moms (especially in my homeschooling world) would be horrified if I ever admitted that I liked [socializing with] certain non-Christian 'groups' better."

Yet another echoed my own feelings, saying she struggles the most with "groups of mothers at playgroups and library story time. Even though many of them are probably experiencing similar difficulties in terms of mothering, identity, and work/life balance, somehow I always feel like I need to differentiate myself from them." I share her desire to break away from what the world sees only as "the herd." We want to show others that we are special—when everyone assumes we're just other "ordinary" moms.

It's no mystery why moms feel lonely. My Big Mom Group characterized the fallout from not fitting in as isolation, alienation, frustration, being misunderstood, stressed, insecure, disconnected, guilty (of course), anxious, judged, and dark.

While each of these is troubling, talk of "darkness" gets *really* troubling. In her very honest chapter called "The Truth about Depression," my friend Carla writes:

> It's interesting to me that one element of being a "good" mother
> is to nurture the God-given gifts in our children and see them as
> individuals for whom God has a unique purpose, while at the
> same time expecting women to fit into one specific mold of
> mothering. When we dismiss a woman's unhappiness with a role
> that she is not allowed to tailor to her own gifts, we essentially
> send the message that the person God created her to be, the life
> she senses God leading her toward, is somehow flawed. Talk
> about depressing.[7]

When I first read that paragraph, I cried for a long time. One, because Carla's words spoke a truth from God that touched on something I myself had long felt but that seemed understood by no one else. Two, okay, I had just had another baby and was *totally* hormonal. Three, because I didn't know until reading this chapter in her book that she had suffered from depression. Carla is a good friend with whom I worked for years—closely! We traveled together on business, laughed together at the office, and shared some of my favorite life moments together (which mostly include laughing while traveling, actually). But as well as I had once known her, I hadn't known her at all.

So I cried for Carla, I cried for me, and I cried for all the other moms who've felt so hurt and lost and dark because we don't fit some stupid ideal. Because we've got these fake I.D.'s.

But Isn't This So Selfish?

No matter what struggles we may face, we do have voices, and we do have power—to change the way we're seen and known.

So why don't we? Especially with such dark consequences as depression, isolation, alienation, and loneliness, why haven't we tackled our identity crises? I think the answer is simple and totally understandable, to a point. It seems so *selfish* and so *silly* to be worrying about these things. I mean, come on! There are wars and famines and earthquakes! In light of such catastrophes, it seems like we moms should be able to deal with our own identities!

Yes, raising children is a high honor and calling. I'm fully on board with that. Any mom would do anything for her kids—because they *are* worth it. But giving up our identities isn't doing anything for our kids. In fact, it does them a disservice.

Worrying about who we are and who God made us to be *isn't* selfish and doesn't mean we're sacrificing our children on the altar of the god Self. To the contrary, wanting to be known and loved as our true selves, as the complete, gifted, purposed women God created us to be, is a God-honoring way to live. In fact, it's a reflection of God (we'll get to this in the next chapter). We should care about our identities *because* we care about our children, because we love our families, because we love our neighbors, and because we love God.

Speaking of whom, let's move on to the next chapter and see what God has to say about his identity. That truth will help us understand what he thinks about ours.

QUESTIONS FOR REFLECTION AND DISCUSSION

- In what way(s) does the "mom label" fit you best? In what ways does your real identity vary from the traditional "mom definition"?
- How has being mislabeled affected your life?
- When have you experienced someone thinking you didn't have a brain because you were a mom? What was the outcome?
- Does being concerned about others' knowing your true identity seem selfish to you? Why or why not?

CHAPTER 3

Take Your Cues
from God

Learn about yourself based on God's
approach to revealing himself

For the five years that I've been the mother of preschoolers, my attendance at the MOPS (Mothers of Preschoolers) group at my church has been what one might call *spotty*. This was due partly to nap schedules, partly to work schedules, and partly to laziness on winter mornings. (Dragging two crabby kids and me out the door when it's fifteen degrees outside? I don't think so!)

But during a rough pregnancy with my third child I realized I needed empathetic ears, so you couldn't keep me away from MOPS meetings! I needed other moms who would understand my pregnancy-induced exhaustion and the shooting pains and nausea I endured while attempting to care for a toddler and a preschooler. Not that my husband wasn't good in this regard. But his empathy quotient lost something when he passed a kidney stone and the nurse (though I can think of another word that suits her better) at his doctor's office went gaga over his "toughness" in withstanding the pain without medication. She actually said to him, "Everyone knows passing a kidney stone is worse than childbirth."

Really?

It's a good thing I'm not a violent person. I know it hurt and all—and I felt terrible for Rafi while he was going through it. But what kind of self-respecting woman tells a man whose wife is having a horrific pregnancy that his kidney stone is more painful than childbirth?

So anyway, I needed empathy and listening ears, so I started going to MOPS again. But when I got there, I found out God had other ideas for me. In fact, one of the unexpected blessings was a discussion on how God shows and tells us who he really is. In other words, how God expresses his true identity. This was a revelation, because I finally realized that God has established the model for how we are to make ourselves known to others.

Looking at God's I.D.

One day my boss handed me a copy of Carolyn Custis James's book *When Life and Beliefs Collide,* from which I discovered the value and simplicity of theology. Carolyn boils theology down to this: it's about knowing God, and as we seek to know who God is, we study theology. Since you and I want to be known, we need to spend time getting to know the One whose image we bear, the One who made us worthy of being known. We need to understand how God makes himself known.

We also need to clear away any nagging feelings that our concern with our identities is somehow selfish and lacking in godliness. This isn't true—yet Christian moms are frequently told that we shouldn't be concerned with who we are aside from our relationship to God, our husbands, and our children. Scripture shows us that getting to know ourselves and making ourselves known has its foundation in God's self-revelation.

God has given us a lot of ways to get to know him: creation, the Bible, the Holy Spirit, prayer, other Christians. It's obvious that God longs for us—the people he loves—to know him, understand him, and experience him. He's a one-of-a-kind God, so he goes out of his way to help us get to know him in all his uniqueness.

Back in theology classes in college—and probably in church cate-
chism class, though I don't remember because I skipped a lot!—we
called the first way God reveals himself *general revelation,* meaning he
shows himself in creation and it's available for all to see. Then there is
special revelation, referring to the ways God shows who he is through the
Bible, through miracles, through the work of his Spirit, and through the
incarnation of Jesus.

In this chapter we'll look at knowing God through the works of his
hands, through his names, through his story, and through his relationships. I hope you'll see that your identity is of prime importance to God.
If you have doubts, consider the ways he chooses to communicate who
he is to those he loves. An authentic relationship is based, in part, on a
clear understanding of a person's true identity.

The Works of His Hands

I'm so glad Romans 1:20 says what it does: "Since the creation of the
world God's invisible qualities—his eternal power and divine nature—
have been clearly seen, being understood from what has been made." It
goes on to say that we are, then, "without excuse." If this verse weren't
in the New Testament, I'd feel like a heretic admitting that as I've looked
around at God's vast and varied creation, he has always struck me as a
bit, well, flashy. You know what I mean? Our God knows how to promote himself! If you're out there looking for him, he's tough to miss.
Hallelujah for that!

God is there in the stuff you always hear people talk about: *How can
you look at the Grand Canyon and not see God? How can you look into your
new baby's eyes and not see God? How can you watch the sun set over a
peaceful bay and not see God?*

And it's all true. We get to know God, see his "invisible qualities," his
creativity, his sense of order, and his love of beauty through the artistry and
invention of his creation. We get to know God by his craftsmanship.

I've been a Christian since I was a young girl, so I've been experiencing this truth for most of my life. However, my most distinct—and perhaps profound—memory of getting to know God through creation came the summer after I graduated high school. I headed off to a Colorado Challenge youth-group retreat. I was sitting on the side of what I remember to be a pine-spotted, jagged mountain. (I'm from Chicago so it could've been a hill for all I know.) I was on an "assignment" to discover something about God from nature. In the brisk summer air, as the wind zipped through the pines, I looked around awestruck at the beautiful brown and green and blue panorama before me. I remember thinking I *felt God* as I sat on that mountain. So I wrote in my journal that in nature you sense how big God is, how imaginative he is, how much he must love us to make these mountains for us to enjoy, and that you *feel* God in nature. But then the cynical teenager in me wrote these words: *but it's easy to feel God in the mountains.*

While I was being snide and cynical, the words tell the truth. It *is* easy to feel or know God in the mountains. Almost too easy. You know what I mean?

As powerful as the presence of God is when I marvel at his handiwork while I'm crossing the Mississippi River or hiking in the Rocky Mountains, or as much as I can learn about his power and goodness standing with my feet in soft sand at the edge of the Atlantic Ocean or swimming with my kids in Lake Michigan, God calls us to seek him beyond the "biggies" in creation. He wants us to go beyond the obvious, to dive (literally) below the waterline, peek behind the hedges and look under rocks, and reach into the sky to experience him and what he can do. He wants us to pay attention to the little things, the most obscure details, to see the range of his work and to know him better.

If you lived in my neighborhood during a recent summer, God's craftsmanship and deliberateness were apparent in the bizarre, vibrant beauty of the millions of cicadas that made themselves at home in the

Midwest. Every seventeen years, these clunky, locustlike creatures crawl out of the dirt, climb up trees and fence posts, and shed their creepy tan husks (and leave them clinging there). Then they tumble back to the ground, grab hold of a blade of grass, and lay wait until they can fly and mate. Their screamy mating calls (best described by my plumber as "alien spacecraft descending") drown out the regular summer sounds of kids playing, water splashing, and crickets chirping. Once they learn to fly, these hulking bugs dart all around, swarming you and your kids as you walk under trees, crash-landing in your hair or calmly clinging to your clothes. (If you're bad with bugs, stay out of my town in 2024 when they come back!)

But as unnerving as they are *en masse,* when you spot one alone, with its gold-trimmed, lacey wings perched up, red eyes nearly sparkling against its dull black body, brown sticky legs grabbing and crawling, you receive an invitation to get to know God a little better. If you accept that invitation, you get to experience a creation that is shared by so few, so seldom on earth. It's remarkable really.

When I was out there with my kids—who could've spent all day chasing cicadas with butterfly nets, collecting them in twig-filled buckets, and flipping over the poor saps—I *felt* God. When my kids would ask questions, which I rarely could answer, like "Why'd they come out?" "Why are their eyes red?" "Why are their feet sticky?" "Why do they die?" it got me thinking more about the kind of God who'd create such a peculiar thing.

These off-putting creatures, who spend sixteen years and forty-seven weeks of every seventeen years deep within trees and below flower beds, give us a glimpse into a God who wants us to know about the things that dwell beneath. We see a Creator who makes not only big and beautiful, but also underground and ugly. He's a Creator who does things in both shiny and dull, in both cuddly and creepy. And because it's all from God's hand, it's all worth knowing.

God reveals himself not just in the "easy" or the obvious, but in the largely unseen, in the stuff you need to dig for, reach toward, wait around for, and even swat at.

His Names

If through creation we get to know the artistry and wonder of God's hands, in the Bible we get to know the love, strength, grace, wisdom, and justice of God's heart and mind.

What's amazing to me is that if you read nothing else from Scripture except the names by which God is called and how he is described, you'd get a solid sense of who he is. I'm not advocating the "Name-Only Bible"—we need the whole story—but God and those he inspired to write his Word captured his essence so beautifully in so few words. Take a look at how he's described just in the first few psalms:

a shield (3:3)
my King (5:2)
Most High (9:2)
a refuge (14:6)
a rock (18:2)
a fortress (18:2)
a deliverer (18:2)
a shepherd (23: 1)
the Lord Almighty (24:10)
a Savior (25:5)
a light (27:1)

Here are more from the gospel of John:

the Word (1:1)
the Son (1:14, MSG)

the Father (1:14)
Rabbi (1:38)
spirit (4:24)
the bread of life (6:35)
Son of Man (6:62)
the resurrection and the life (11:25)
the way and the truth (14:6)

God uses these names and terms—and many others—to reveal himself eloquently and engagingly, yet succinctly. He could have decided just to be known as God. Period. But he loves us and wants to make himself fully known. These names and descriptions help us relate to him and bring him close. They make him real to us. They stir up images that drive us to think more deeply about who he is.

The names also comfort and attend to us. Lately, the stresses of life have pushed pretty hard on my shoulders. Some nights, as I have prayed for relief from my worries, I've found deliverance through the image of the Rock. The visual of me adrift and sinking in stormy waters (which is how I sometimes feel) and reaching out and clinging to a big Rock gives me hope and strength that could only come from God.

Then there's the superfreaky-fit woman I once heard describing her encounter with the Bread of Life while she stood in front of her open fridge, looking for comfort in leftovers. Apparently, whenever she's worn thin from too little sleep and too much work and tempted to "reach for the carbs," she's reminded of the Bread of Life whom she should really be looking to for sustenance.

While I can't imagine that God called himself the Bread of Life just so this woman would find the strength to avoid an unhealthy snack, neither do I think that when God offered all these descriptions of himself he was trying simply to mix it up linguistically. God reveals himself with a purpose. He offers so many descriptions to show us essential aspects of his character, his wisdom, his love, his goodness: his whole identity. In wanting to be fully known, he uses explicit, concrete language to describe what he does, his relationship to others, and how he thinks and feels.

His Story

The simplest description I've heard of the Bible (and I've heard a lot of them) is that it's the story of God and his people. God's story has it all: a beautiful beginning, a heartbreaking tragedy, a compelling plot, intrigue and subplots and suspense, an eternity-altering climax, and a satisfying denouement—not to mention the promise of a powerful sequel! Within its pages you find action, romance, mystery, poetry, wisdom, and even a little bathroom humor. (Check out Judges 3:12–30, the story of the left-handed judge Ehud. Your kids will love you for this. Plus, the gruesome ending will keep you from reaching for those carbs!)

But of course, the Bible is more than a literary masterpiece. The story of God and his people changes lives through the saga of God's love, his sacrifice, his grace, and our redemption. And for those who accept the story's conclusion—that Jesus died for the forgiveness of our sins—it's a book that helps transform us. It makes us more like the Author by making us new creations in Christ (see 2 Corinthians 5:17).

Part of our transformation to become more like Christ comes about from knowing God's story. Through the Scriptures we get to know God by reading how he reacts to obedience and disobedience, how he exhibits justice and mercy, how he gets angry but doesn't sin, how he loves us so much that he sacrificed his precious Son. In his Word, we read stories and instructions that get us right into the heart and mind of God.

As he takes us through the history of his people, God is also showing us who he is. Sharing experiences, stories, and history are essential ways God invites us to get to know him.

His Relationships

What's weird about getting to know God through his relationships is that to know God is to know him *as* a relationship; i.e., the Trinity. He is Father. He is Son. He is Holy Spirit. All three in relationship with one another. And each of these shows us an important "angle" of our God.

While it may take some mental gymnastics—not to mention huge leaps of faith—to imagine God the Father sending God the Son to earth and then, thirty-three years later leaving God the Holy Spirit to live in our hearts, can you think of a more loving, personal, and intimate way of making himself known? What better way could he have used to show himself to us than by making himself human to live among us (and then to die for us!) and then leaving his Spirit to live within us?

When God became human and walked, ate, slept, and talked with his people, he showed that physical, emotional, and familial relationships matter to God. These same relationships help reveal and describe God. He took this loving, and humbling, step of making himself known not just as a far-off, heaven-dwelling Supreme Being, but as a Son of Man, the "step-Son" of a simple carpenter (who came from kings) and Son of a courageous, faithful, obedient teenage mother who was chosen for an astounding journey.

Within these relationships, we see God briefly as a little boy—first a baby worshiped by shepherds and wise men, heralded by angels, and (we can assume) nursed sweetly by his loving mom and cradled by his faithful, earthly father. Then we see him as a bit of a renegade twelve-year-old who (without sinning, though to be honest, this seems to come quite close) gives his parents a heart attack when he lags behind at the temple instead of journeying home with his clan. In these stories, we see pictures of classic family relationships at work.

And as an adult, the God-man related still with his mother and brothers and his friends as well as interacting with "strangers." We see

Jesus desiring the company of others—as well as getting time alone. With Jesus, we get to see the Heavenly Father up close and in the flesh. We get to know him in a personal, friendly, and "family" way.

But perhaps what blows my mind the most about God and relationships is just how much he *wants* one with us. He sends us an invitation to come to his house. And more incredibly, he does this despite knowing us as we really are. Despite knowing that we are disobedient even when we know better and that we complain in the face of his goodness. But this is God's grace, and once you feel it, this grace makes God—and a relationship with him—irresistible. Who doesn't want to hang out with Someone who knows *everything* about her and loves her still?

Once we accept the invitation to live our lives with God and in his grace, we get to know him in the most intimate way imaginable as the Spirit leads us, guides us, comforts us, transforms us. Really, aside from Jesus' rising from the dead, this has to be the most difficult-to-believe aspect of the Christian faith in the eyes of a nonbeliever. But for those of us who know this part of God—and who have grown in him because of the Holy Spirit's presence in our lives—it becomes not weird but wonderful.

One of my favorite hymns is Keith Green's song "There Is a Redeemer." I've loved it since my parents would play the record album in our living room when I was a girl. Now we sing it in church, and it packs a punch every time. The whole song actually relates a bit to this chapter, but in particular I keep thinking of the chorus, where Green thanks the Father for the Son and then, for

> ...leaving your Spirit
> till the work on earth is done.[1]

Aside from the work of the Holy Spirit, essential to telling the world about Jesus and his saving love is that you use the gifts God gave you and you seek to be the person he created you to be. Part of fulfilling that calling is making yourself known as you really are. You need to let others know the complete person God made you to be. And God, by revealing himself in a rich variety of ways, has shown you how to do just that. (We'll delve much more deeply into this in chapter 10.)

QUESTIONS FOR REFLECTION AND DISCUSSION

▢ Of the various ways God reveals himself, which are the most meaningful to you? Why?

▢ Why do you think God goes to such great lengths to make himself known? What does that tell you about the importance of revealing yourself to others?

▢ In what ways have you gotten to know God through the works of his hands? How do your own creations help others get to know you?

▢ Which of the names or descriptions of God particularly resonate with you? Why?

▢ What names do other people use to identify you (nicknames, given name, titles such as *mom, aunt, daughter, sister, friend*)? How do these names help others get to know you more completely?

▢ Think of your favorite story (or stories) from the Bible. How does it help you get to know and love God? What is your favorite story from your life? Have you shared it with the people who are close to you?

CHAPTER 4

Why God Cares About Who You Are

God, more than anyone else, wants to know you

One of the toughest challenges of motherhood (or any "hood" for that matter!) is filtering the constant feedback you receive. If you pay too much attention to much of what you hear, you'll want to either turn in your resignation or punch somebody. I don't recommend either. So, in search of a healthier perspective, I asked some mom friends what they do when they hear yet again that their value as women is pretty much limited to what they do for their families.

When I asked my friend Carla if she'd ever doubted whether God made her special or equipped her with special gifts—outside of motherhood—she replied almost instantly with a big "No!" She'd never doubted that she had much to contribute to the world beyond her family. I asked about the times when she had felt she was specially gifted.

She wrote back, "I felt that way when I worked at camp. It just came so easily for me—making up games, hanging out with kids, problem solving, etc. It was a job that pulled all my creative and relationship skills to the forefront, and it was a wonderful feeling to be, as my friend Thom, says, 'firing on all cylinders.'"

Another friend told me about times when she felt she was doing exactly what God created her to do. I would assume that just about every

Christian woman has had this experience of being specially created to make a unique contribution to the world.

I grew up secure in the knowledge that God created me special, that he gave *me* certain gifts and abilities, in a particular combination, and that he loved me just the way he made me. (Thank God for this, and thanks, Mom and Dad, for teaching me this!) I never doubted that God cared about my identity.

That is, until I talked to a kind, godly, older woman whom I'll call Candy. One day, Candy and I were chatting about motherhood. As I blathered on about my own identity issues as well as those of many of the moms I knew, she nodded along.

"Yes," she said. "I remember those days well. It's rough!"

So I continued on with some ideas I had about how to help women find their full identities and to allow God to use them in a greater variety of ways. I expected an enthusiastic response. Instead, Candy stopped me, put her hand on my arm, and said, "Remember, Caryn, God gave you these kids for a reason. You've got to stop worrying about *you*. You can do that later. You need to worry about *them* now."

She wasn't telling me this in a wise, grandmotherly way. She actually seemed agitated by my talk about the importance of a mother's identity. I don't know if you've ever been called a bad mom to your face, but I'm almost certain at some point you've heard this same message.

This is why another friend replied to my first e-mail, saying she knew that God cares about her identity, but she still hears the little voice in the back of her head that whispers, *Come on. You think God cares about your special gifts? No. He just wants you to raise godly kids. Stop being so selfish and worrying about your identity.*

Carla would argue that the little voice is merely echoing the message we keep hearing. "So many [Christians] can't accept that a woman can love her children like crazy and still want to do more than devote herself to them 24/7," Carla said. "One doesn't exclude the other."

Candy is an example of a woman who bought into this one-sided thinking. She almost had me believing that to be concerned with my own identity meant I wasn't concerned about my kids. That's why being a mom who wants to be used by God in a wide variety of ways can *feel* so selfish even when we know it's not. But because there are many well-meaning Christians who really do think moms should be happy to invest everything they have in their children, I think we moms need to explore the will of God for women whom he has blessed with children. God cares about us as *people,* not just as mothers.

The Bible Tells Me So

At the heart of this whole identity issue is our simple desire to be known and to not feel alone. We could simplify the matter and try to explain away the struggle by saying, "If we're made in the image of a God who wants to be known, it's okay for us to want to be known as well."[1]

Author Sharon Hersh captures this beautifully: "Your longing for relationships—a longing that whispers, *Ask me, notice me, enjoy me, pursue me, love me, and stay with me*—is nothing to be ashamed of. Your longing to belong is a reflection of the image of God. He gave you this longing not only to transform you more into his image, but as a force to draw you to others. Your loneliness can become the ground of fruitful relationships if you recognize it, respond to it, and rely on the One who created you for relationships."[2]

If you want to be assured that you are special and precious to God, that you weren't just stamped out and issued a random uterus to make yourself useful, you need to look no further than David's beautiful Psalm 139. In his words we read of a God who loves us, knows us, makes each of us special, and wants to hang out with us! If you're not familiar with it, here it is. (And even if you are, it's worth a reread!)

O LORD, you have searched me
and you know me.

You know when I sit and when I rise;
    you perceive my thoughts from afar.
You discern my going out and my lying down;
    you are familiar with all my ways.
Before a word is on my tongue
    you know it completely, O LORD.

You hem me in—behind and before;
    you have laid your hand upon me.
Such knowledge is too wonderful for me,
    too lofty for me to attain.

Where can I go from your Spirit?
    Where can I flee from your presence?
If I go up to the heavens, you are there;
    if I make my bed in the depths, you are there.
If I rise on the wings of the dawn,
    if I settle on the far side of the sea,
even there your hand will guide me,
    your right hand will hold me fast.

If I say, "Surely the darkness will hide me
    and the light become night around me,"
even the darkness will not be dark to you;
    the night will shine like the day,
    for darkness is as light to you.

For you created my inmost being;
    you knit me together in my mother's womb.
I praise you because I am fearfully and wonderfully made;
    your works are wonderful,
    I know that full well.

My frame was not hidden from you
> when I was made in the secret place.
When I was woven together in the depths of the earth,
> your eyes saw my unformed body.
All the days ordained for me
> were written in your book
> before one of them came to be.

How precious to me are your thoughts, O God!
> How vast is the sum of them!
Were I to count them,
> they would outnumber the grains of sand.
When I awake,
> I am still with you.
> (Psalm 139:1–18)

"But, wait!" you might say. "This is *King David* we're talking about. A man after God's *own heart*. A man from whom *Jesus* descended. So of course, God knit *him* special. Of course, God was with *him* in the heavens and in the depths. Of course, God ordained *his* days. But what about me?"

So, what about you?

I say, if you can believe that God made you more than *just* a mom and if you believe God's Word applies to you, then of course this means you too. Just as God didn't view David as *just* a shepherd, *just* a poet, *just* a king, or *just* a man on the run, God views you as *much* more than any one role.

While perhaps the whole "knitting together" verses are the most famous of this chapter, it's the opener that makes me a little weak in the knees. I almost get misty-eyed when I contemplate the deeper meaning behind God *searching* us and *knowing* us. He knows when we sit and rise. He cares about what we're thinking. He knows our routines.

Think about the people you know that intimately: your spouse, your kids, maybe your closest friend, your parents. We know that much detail only about the people we love deeply—and are interested in the most. It's the same with God. He knows us like that not only because he loves us but because he's vitally, untiringly interested in us. God finds you—as his creation, as his child—interesting and *worth knowing*.

Why shouldn't everyone else?

Jesus Recognizes Your Worth

The Bible is filled with examples of God's intense interest in us, and some of the most poignant interactions involve Jesus.

Since I was a little girl singing "Zacchaeus was a wee little man and a wee little man was he…" in Sunday school, the story of Jesus and the man "who climbed up in a sycamore tree to see what he could see" has been one of my favorites.[3] Since the story was first told to me on 1970s flannelgraphs, I've imagined Jesus, both touched and amused, spotting this crazy guy up in a tree. I can picture Jesus squinting into the sun, pointing his finger at the man who is half-perched, half-dangling in the tree, and saying, "Zacchaeus, get down here—quick. I'm coming to *your* house for dinner." I picture Zacchaeus scurrying down and snatching a few figs out of the tree as he goes—after all, he was a notorious thief, which is why everyone who knew this slimy tax collector was horrified that Jesus would be going to his house.

But as Jesus says at the end of the story, he came to seek out and save the lost.[4] And while he came to die so we can *all* be saved if we accept his gift of grace, time and again we see Jesus reach out to individuals. He shows interest in one person, getting to know that woman or man— sometimes over dinner—as he seeks to save that person.

It's a theme we see repeated again and again: with the prodigal son, in the parables of the lost sheep and the lost coin, with the Samaritan woman at the well. One person is as important to Jesus as the masses.

If you are a follower of Jesus, I'm sure you've experienced his interest in you, one-on-one. I imagine you have had your share of Zacchaeus moments—when Jesus pointed at you as you clung haplessly to something, hoping to catch a glimpse of a savior. That's when he called you by name and asked to spend some time with you.

When Jesus shows a personal interest in you, it changes your life. It's those personal encounters with a God who loves us and meets us where we are—even up a tree (or more often up a creek!)—and wants to *know* us, intimately, that change us. It would be wrong to keep others from getting to know the person you are becoming as God changes you.

Which brings me to our next point.

You, with Purpose

Recently a friend of mine lost her beloved pet bunny. In a lame act of trying to console her, I got out my copy of Randy Alcorn's interesting and life-changing book *Heaven,* which contains words of comfort. On my way to the chapter where he writes beautifully about the probability of a reunion with our pets in the New Earth, I stumbled on another chapter, which included this subhead: "Will We Maintain Our Own Identities [in Heaven]?" Hello!

Since I credit Randy Alcorn's wisdom with curbing my materialism, "curing" me of my lust for a bigger and cooler house, and reassuring me that one day I will indeed get to walk, pet, and snuggle with my beloved dogs again, I stopped to see what he had to say about my identity.

I laughed when I read this: "You will be *you* in heaven. Who else would you be?"[5]

Good question. But I hadn't really thought about it before. I kept reading, and he kept making good points about our identities in eternity.

"If we weren't ourselves in the afterlife," he writes, "then we couldn't be held accountable for what we did in this life. The Judgment would be meaningless. If Barbara is no longer Barbara, she can't be rewarded or held accountable for anything Barbara did.... The doctrines of judgment and eternal rewards depend on people's retaining their distinct identities from this life to the next."[6]

Interesting, huh? While I've spent a lot of time thinking about who we are *now* and *here,* I hadn't paid much attention to the eternal significance of who we are made to be. But who we are *here* on earth has implications for who we are in heaven. And what we *do* as us affects our judgment and reward after this life.

Rick Warren famously starts off *The Purpose Driven Life* with these words: "It's not about you."[7] I agree completely. Our purpose on earth is not to do what pleases us, but what pleases God. So you'd still think this means we should chuck worrying about *who* we are, right? Wrong. Because if we're going to please God on this planet (and for eternity), we need to do it as we are, using everything he gave us and all the ways he equipped us. In that sense, it *is* about you—about you living for God as *you.* There are a bunch of different reasons for this—all good.

Living as God's beloved

When I first asked myself *why* I thought God cared about who I was, the most obvious answer seemed to be that I am his beloved. It came right out of my "mom" heart (you know, the one that helps us understand God's heart).

Asking if God cares about who I am is as needless as asking if *I* care about who my kids are. Do I care if Henrik uses his gifts? Do I care if Greta finds herself held back by stereotypes—told what she can and can't do or be based on her race, sex, or looks? Do I care if anyone ever bothers to get to know the real Fredrik?

Of course! Why? Because I love them. Because I know how wonderful, how interesting, how gifted, and how worth knowing they are. Because they're my children. As their mother who loves them eternally, it's not only my job to help them grow their gifts, but my privilege and joy to watch them use their gifts—and be valued and useful because of them. When my children live and act as the people they were made to be, it honors me as their mom. This has to echo God's heart as my loving Father.

As reflections of Christ

C. S. Lewis wrote: "There is so much of Him that millions and millions of 'little Christs,' all different, will still be too few to express Him fully."[8]

We aren't simply passive image-bearers. As Christians, we are called to express who Christ is. And there are *many* aspects of motherhood that do this well. Embodied in the "perfect" mother—whom most of us aspire to be—is the nature of God. In him we see nurture, love, compassion, understanding, generosity, grace, justice, discipline, wisdom, kindness. I could go on. The things that we all wish we were as mothers are things found in our perfect God. (Okay, so maybe he doesn't have that flat stomach and perky boobs, but you know what I mean.) Good mothers reflect the good nature of our good God.

That said, of course we were born—conceived even—bearing God's image long before we became mothers. And we continue to reflect that image in ways that have nothing to do with motherhood and in ways that only we, as individually gifted and created women, can reflect. If we're not shining, no one is seeing the "little Christ" in us.

As the gifted ones

If you believe part of what makes you distinctly "you" are the gifts God has given you, then you know we're all expected to use our gifts. In Scripture, we see this illustrated in the parable of the talents[9] and spelled out in Luke 12:48: "From everyone who has been given much, much will be demanded; and from the one who has been entrusted with much, much more will be asked."

But my favorite example of God loving to see our individual gifts in action comes from two powerful stories involving Jesus' countercultural and history-altering interactions with Mary of Bethany. The first one takes place in Luke 10:38–42, the famous story of our eager-to-learn Mary and her hostess-with-the-mostest sister, Martha. While Mary learns at Jesus' feet, Martha, of course, remains in the kitchen getting the food prepared and complaining about Mary's not helping.

Though I've read this story—along with reading and hearing *about it*—a million times, when I first wrote about this in a Bible study for ChristianBibleStudies.com, the story touched me in a whole new way.

I wrote: "Mary does the unthinkable: she brazenly steps out of her place and comes crashing through a stereotype. All in the name of Jesus. In her defiance of expectations and the subsequent critique from her sister and defense from Jesus, she ends up getting ministered to by her Lord—and ultimately ministering to thousands of years of believers."[10]

But beyond that, for the first time I really saw a Jesus who welcomed this woman who brought nothing but herself and offered her worship and adoration. Maybe she hated cooking; maybe she wasn't a gifted hostess; maybe she was a curious woman who loved to learn—and up until this point had probably never been allowed to. Certainly not among men! Jesus let Mary be who she was created to be.[11]

It's amazing. And then he does it again. In Mark 14:3–9, Mary of Bethany famously (as Jesus prophesied it would be!) broke her alabaster jar and lavishly anointed Jesus with expensive perfume. While others found nothing better to do than point out her wastefulness, Jesus praised her gift and highlighted its importance and eternal significance.

The trouble with Mary was that she didn't fit. God had given her attributes and longings that didn't square with first-century expectations of a woman. But the blessing is that Jesus welcomed, rejoiced in, and defended who she was. He encouraged her right to be different, along with the purpose for her differences. He knew why she was the woman she was, and he was glad when she offered that to him.[12]

This passage is good news for any woman who feels at times like she doesn't fit into a role or an environment (and who of us doesn't?). Jesus welcomes you and your gifts.

As parts of the Body

Before my sophomore year at the best college in the country, Calvin College,[13] our resident advisor (RA) apparently decided our hall theme would be "We Are the Body [of Christ]." So on the first day of school, each set of roommates on our floor was greeted by a laminated skeletal body part that doubled as a message board stuck on our doors. Some of the girls had arm bones. Some had the skull. Some had foot bones. My roommate and I had the pelvis. Picture it: a big old pelvic bone slapped on our door.

Our RA told us later that she actually *prayed* about who should get the pelvis. She said she sensed a "peace" about its recipients being Betty and me—that we wouldn't be offended. She sensed correctly. Not only were we not offended, we were endlessly amused. I *still* have that pelvis message board tucked away in my college-memories box. It made me laugh every day I saw it—as did the thought of random people scribbling notes on our pelvis—and it still makes me laugh now.

In fact, I can't hear a message (or a song, as it were) about being the body of Christ in this world without imagining myself as the pelvis. Which *is* weird, I realize, but it's that image—of me as the pelvis—that has helped broaden my view of what it means to be a part of the Body.

While you'll probably never hear anybody sing or preach about being the pelvis of Christ to the world (at least I hope not), each part— no matter how weird or amusing—is important. Each has purpose. While the "hands" or "feet" get most of the glory for doing things for the kingdom of God—we need the clavicles; we need the collarbones; we *desperately* need the funny bones. And, by George, we need a good pelvis!

Hear me out: I once heard David Batstone, president and founder of Not for Sale, a campaign to end human trafficking, define an *abolitionist* as "anyone who acts in any way to contribute to the freedom of another person." I love that. Because when I think of an abolitionist—someone who's putting an end to modern-day slavery—I've got to be honest: I'm picturing the "arms" and "legs" who storm back alleys in Bangkok, run out of brothels with enslaved kids under their arms, and lock up the people who held them hostage. I don't think of the "fingers" who write checks to support those missions or the "pelvises" who might, right this minute, be sitting back and writing about it in a book. But according to Batstone, *every* part, purposed by God, matters in the campaign.

Lest any of this talk of our importance go to our heads, I'll mention this one thing (but use the words of Tracey Bianchi). Tracey is a mother, speaker, and former director of young adults and families at Christ Church of Oak Brook (Illinois), and she captured what I want to say beautifully: "The moment we begin to think that we are indispensable to the kingdom of God is the moment our heads become too big to cram through the door, thus rendering us useless. The reality is that indeed someone else *can* serve in your position. However, God called *you* to do it. He invited *you* to serve and lead in this specific capacity. He designed you with a gift set and a passion that no one else on the planet can bring."[14]

And that's why I love this story of a woman who has used her passions and gift set in a way I don't think anyone else on the planet has done: Sybil MacBeth is a mother, a mathematician, a dancer, a doodler, and a pastor's wife. While I'm sure God is using her other gifts plenty in this world, it's the *doodler* in her that's making some serious waves. In her book *Praying in Color: Drawing a New Path to God,* she shares the profound experience she's had in offering God her doodled prayers. I discovered her in an article in *Christianity Today.* Here's what I read:

> Going to the back porch, she doodled a random shape and
> wrote a name in its center. [MacBeth said,] "The name be-
> longed to one of the people on my prayer list. I stayed
> with the same shape and the name, adding detail and color
> to the drawing. Each dot, each line, and each stroke of color
> became another moment of time spent with the person in
> the center."
>
> When she sensed the time was right, she moved to another
> part of the page and drew another shape and put another name
> in its middle. She embellished it with lines, dots, colors. She
> continued drawing new shapes and names until her friends
> and family formed a colorful community of designs. "To my
> surprise," she writes, "I had not just doodled—I had prayed."[15]

This story connected with me right away—as someone who gets spacey while praying, someone who has *tried* to write out prayers (I am a writer after all!) but gets bored, and someone who prays best in fits and starts, as my mom would say.

So what's my point? That God made this woman a doodler—and gave her the gift of the doodler prayers—to share with others. Since discovering this little doodle "trick," my prayer life has improved and I've gotten closer with God. Who knows how many other people who struggle with prayer have been helped and inspired to pray in some creative way or even to look at their gifts through new eyes? Sybil MacBeth is touching lives and impacting the world because she's a doodler. A *doodler!* That's the pelvis of Christ at work if I've ever seen one.

That's why God cares who you are.

QUESTIONS FOR REFLECTION AND DISCUSSION

- Have you ever doubted whether God equipped you with special gifts? If so, when? If not, why do you suppose that is?
- Have you experienced a time when you've wondered if God meant for you to be a mom, period?
- How difficult (or easy) is it for you to believe that God finds you interesting and worth knowing?
- Think of a time when you felt like you didn't fit. How does it feel to know that who you are always fits with Jesus?
- Which part of the body of Christ do you see yourself as? Why?

CHAPTER 5

How Moms Are Left Homeless in God's House

Of all people, Christians should know the truth about moms

If God is so heavily invested in who you are in particular, rather than relegating you to an amorphous blob of Christian moms, then shouldn't God's people be taking your full identity much more seriously?

It reminds me of a story. A friend from Colorado was attempting to merge onto the highway. As he came roaring down the on-ramp, he noticed a big old sedan in the right-hand lane of the highway, heading his same direction but failing to scooch over into the left lane.

After nearly slamming on his brakes to get behind the other car, he noticed the back was plastered with bumper stickers that identified the motorists as lovers of God and of America. "They love America," my friend told me. "I guess they just don't care all that much for Americans."

You know, that's a lot like the way many Christians—not to mention the institutional church—react to moms. They love the "idea" of motherhood and on many levels they recognize the value of moms, but when it comes to dealing with an actual mom who doesn't want to volunteer for the nursery or the hospitality committee, they don't know how to react.

It's easy to put motherhood on a pedestal, in part because that keeps moms at a distance. But when you have to deal with a flesh-and-blood mother who wants to exercise the nonmothering gifts that God has loaded her with, things can get awkward really fast. And I don't mean just for the mislabeled mom. It gets uncomfortable for the church as well.

With all the mislabeling and false assumptions, it's no surprise that the moms I interviewed, chatted with, and heard from on my blog often said it's at church where they feel least like themselves. They aren't allowed to be themselves, they don't feel accepted, and they can't find a way to fit in. Some of the prevalent attitudes in the church are hurting a lot of moms, and something needs to change. But this leads to a second issue: what to do about the blame-the-church factor.

Shouldn't We Blame the Church?

The day my friend Carla received a contract offer to write a book *(The Myth of the Perfect Mother)*, she went out to lunch with work friends to celebrate the deal. That's when she ran into a man we both really like and admire. When she told him the good news about the book and gave him a brief synopsis, he rolled his eyes and said, "Just what we need, another book blaming the church."

Ever since, Carla has hoped he was joking—but deep inside she doesn't think he was. Whether he was kidding or not, his comment touches on a prevalent sentiment: people (at least churchgoers) are tired of "the church" getting blamed for everything from global warming to the oil crisis to world hunger to teenagers engaging in oral sex. I totally get this.

But let's be honest. Churches and organized religion have hurt a lot of people in a lot of ways. From the Crusades to slavery to child sex abuse to hundreds of years of misogyny, churches have failed to live up to God's standards. And moms are far from the only people being hurt. It's a major reason given whenever people say they don't believe in God or they hate Christians and the church.

So it comes as no surprise that this is also a major reason that a lot of moms hate church. While Christians love to rhapsodize about one role that is fulfilled exclusively by women (motherhood, of course)—and ironically, to the detriment of childless women—Christians have done a lousy job elevating the other roles of women. In an effort to glorify the family, churches have forgotten that God has other purposes for women. I could go on a real blame tear—as I feel the wounds as deeply as anyone.

But as much as I'd like to blame the church, I can't get it out of my head that *I* am the church; *we* are the church! While I can't attack women who lived in times when they were powerless to make a change—or those who live in places today where they're powerless—I'm not one of them. I have a voice and influence and intelligence and passion. And so do you.

Statistically speaking, women make up about 60 percent of overall church membership in the United States. But even if we represented only 10 percent, we can't blame anyone but ourselves. If moms are stuck in stereotypes, and if women are being left on the fringes, it's because we've allowed it to happen.

I'm not blaming us for the past, but today we can change things. I know, I know. The last thing we moms need is more blame and guilt (we'll work through this in the next chapter). But if we want churches to value and love women as God's creations and not as a role within the family context, we've got to be on the forefront. We can't keep griping among ourselves (though I do consider "martyr" to be one of my gifts). We can't just keep pointing fingers at, say, the men. Because if we're just pointing fingers and not pointing out the problem, the men (and I mean no offense here, fellas) probably don't know there *is* a problem. And what if they do and they're simply ignoring it? Well, all the more reason we've got to move some mountains ourselves (with God's help).

I point out weaknesses and blind spots as a sister in Christ, as part of the body of Christ, as a flawed member of a flawed Christian community that I love and, I think, that loves me (or at least did up until this chapter!). Let's get to it.

The Word on the Street

Last summer I asked a few women what role the church has played in their identity crises. Talk about opening the floodgates! Here's what I learned or was reminded of:

Maggie asked the head of her parachurch organization about working flex hours after her baby was born. He told her to "forget this career stuff—you're a mom now." In the time it took him to utter those words, Maggie toppled from confident, productive, passionate employee to demoralized and demotivated employee. Nice.

Carrie felt like she was sinking under the weight of all the things her church said a mom should be. Church teachings had convinced her that she was a terrible mother, which she is sure contributed to her depression. Though her depression has lifted—and her church home has changed—she still can't shake the sense of failure, which grows out of her inability to meet the long list of a church's unrealistic expectations. Ouch.

Kris stopped attending gatherings with a small group of Christian married couples because it made her feel more lonely, not more connected. Group members would regularly ask her husband about his life and dreams, but Kris only got asked about her kids. She felt invisible, got fed up, and quit. Great.

Sharon won't go back to a church she used to attend because the mothers' group—which the pastor described as a "great fit for moms like you"—spends most of its time doing crafts, talking about new stores and shopping, and griping about husbands who don't make enough money. "Not such a great fit for a mom like me at all," she said. (Makes you wonder why her pastor thought of her as petty, materialistic, and shallow.) She doesn't go to any church now because she thinks Christian women "don't think." Sad.

And then there are the comments sent to GiftedForLeadership.com in response to articles we've done on women's ministry, women and the church, or gender in general. Every time we post a blog on these topics, we get flooded with comments. Here's a typical response:

> After the birth of my second child I expressed my struggle with this identity issue to some friends and fellow staff members of our church. They suggested I see a counselor. They believed what I was feeling was so "outside the norm" that I needed professional help.
>
> Thankfully, the woman I saw for counseling struggled with many of the same issues earlier in her life. She and I met for a few weeks to talk through how I was feeling. At our first meeting she pronounced me normal but said everyone can benefit from a little counseling....
>
> The point I'm trying to make is that in the church I believe women are silenced into saying they're happy with stay-at-home motherhood.[1]

Talk to three moms, and you'll find at least one (and more likely two or three) who have been hurt by the church's tendency to redefine women after they become moms. It's as if God created this phenomenal woman in the womb, but then when she gets a baby in her own womb, God suddenly changes his mind about who he intended her to be. The intentions of Christians are no doubt good ones—to make mothers feel valued and significant in a world that often degrades the contribution of mothers. But in our zeal to honor moms, we tend to dishonor women. In our attempts to create "community" based on convenient group-ings—by age, gender, marital status, and so forth—we leave plenty of women on the outside looking in. And too often we don't even notice the disastrous results. Moms are suffering under outdated (were they ever true?) perceptions of who we are and what we do, what we need and how we can fit in. In doing so, we kick scores of women to the curb, leaving them more isolated and alone than ever.

Homeless in God's House

In her cross-country travels as a speaker and Christian apologist, Jona-lyn Grace Fincher hears story after story from women—regular, church-going Christians—who complain of feeling lost. Jonalyn has dubbed this a state of "homelessness." So many mothers I've spoken to resonated perfectly with this.

When I mentioned this term to a mom who wished to remain anonymous, she said, "That sounds about right. I mean, I go with my family every Sunday, but they belong there, not me. It's more their house than mine."

These words hit a particularly sensitive nerve in me—and it has nothing to do with *motherhood* actually. Her words bring to mind two of my most shameful memories—and best "life lessons." (I wince every time I think back to these.) These events changed my view of church—and how we see others in church—forever.

The first of the horrid memories happened shortly after Henrik was born. As I stood outside the sanctuary rocking him to sleep one Sunday morning, a girl of about fifteen walked out to get a drink of water. She had on one of those short, tight, midriff-baring shirts with writing across the front that basically said "Trashy" or "Easy"—though I don't remember exactly what the words were. Of course she paired the revealing top with thong-baring, low-waisted jeans. Not exactly the outfit I was brought up to wear to church. Or the one I thought *anyone* ought to wear in church.

So I eyeballed her getup and gave her my best "You've *got* to be kidding" wide-eyed, horrified sneer.

When the girl turned back from getting her drink and smiled at me, I still had my sneer on. Her face immediately fell, and she looked down before I could recover. The shame and guilt hit me fast. Somewhere in my chilled insides, I sensed God whisper, *This is* my *house.*

I never saw the girl again. I had never seen her before, so for all I know that might have been her first and last time in church. And there I stood in God's house, indeed, sneering my welcome because this girl's outfit didn't fit *my* idea of "appropriate." It was my first lesson in hospitality God-style, but not my last.

The second time was the day of my brother's wedding. John and my sister-in-law, Gina, got married in a big, old, beautiful-yet-crumbly church in Chicago. We had arrived early to take pictures, and while on an errand up the empty center aisle to find the photographer, I noticed a big, old, crumbly man sleeping in a back pew.

Again, the horrified sneer. "I don't *think* so," I muttered as I turned to find a priest or anyone who could remove the interloper. But in my haste, my heel slipped out from under me. As I steadied myself on a nearby pew back, I caught a glimpse of one of the stations of the cross. When I looked in earnest at the image of Christ, fallen, with the cross on his back, I sensed his voice again—though he sounded much louder this time. (I attribute that to the echo effect in these big old churches.) *You think* you *have any more right to be here than* him? *This is* my *house.* Again, those familiar chilled and shamed insides.

The truth, though? Of course I thought I had more right to be there! I was a bridesmaid (for crying out loud!) scrubbed and beautiful, ready for a wedding. He was a bum (probably drunk), dirty and ugly, ruining a perfect day. (Now you know I'm not very nice.)

But God works with us not-so-nice girls, and in the moments afterward I made some feeble attempts to make amends to the homeless man. Somewhere along the line I must've memorized Matthew 25:35–36 because those words kept echoing in my brain: "I was hungry and you gave me something to eat, I was thirsty and you gave me something to drink, I was a stranger and you invited me in, I needed clothes and you clothed me, I was sick and you looked after me, I was in prison and you came to visit me."

So I did the best I could to treat this man as a guest in God's house. I tucked a note with a hymn lyric and a grocery-store gift card (which I scrounged out of Henrik's diaper bag) into his grungy backpack, and instead of finding a priest to kick him out, I went to find a priest to see if there was something for this man to eat.

The man had disappeared before I found anyone to help (I didn't find the photographer either!). The truth is, my whole life I've held standards for what I thought was appropriate behavior and dress and everything else in God's house. None of my rules have anything to do with what God actually says, but say volumes about how deeply I've been seduced by the things of our culture and human-made traditions.

In fact, according to Matthew 25, my standards were the exact *opposite* of what Jesus says. That girl in the skanky T-shirt was Jesus, and I didn't welcome her. That man sleeping in a pew was Jesus. I did a tad better that time, but only after God tripped me up and made me look Jesus in the face. The words Jesus offers leave no doubt that how we welcome, view, and treat others directly correlates to how we welcome, view, and treat Jesus.

That's why the church needs to care about women, and about moms. Because if we sneer at moms who don't fit our view of what a mom is or does, we sneer at Jesus. If we fail to welcome women as they are into God's house, who will? Since no one should feel homeless while standing in God's house, let's look at how we can extend our hospitality.

Better Etiquette

Having just thrown a party for Fredrik's first birthday, I'm reminded of one thing: I am not a confident, particularly talented hostess. While I love having my family and friends over and I enjoy hosting celebrations as they happen, few of my gifts come into play while entertaining (though I do have pretty plates and make a nice punch). I get stressed out over straightening and cleaning my house; I cannot create good "flow" for the food on the buffet table to save my life; I don't think in terms of centerpieces, flowers, or festive decoration; and I *never* remember to put cream out for the coffee.

My home is not the sort where you can pop by any minute and find it "company ready." Let's just say there's no coffeecake stowed in the freezer and I may need to scoot a few action figures—not to mention a large Rottweiler—off the sofa in the event you do pop by.

But just because I'm not a "perfect hostess" like one of my favorite literary heroines, Virginia Woolf's Mrs. Dalloway, doesn't mean I don't know anything about hospitality or about being attentive. I know that graciousness is at the heart of hospitality and good manners. Grace makes our guests feel welcome and at home.

A good definition of the word *grace* (in the theological sense) is "the freely given, unmerited favor and love of God." A practical understanding of the power and the irresistibility of this grace is the experience of being fully known and yet being loved. That's the grace our Host offers us, and it's the grace we're called to offer others.

This grace doesn't ask a guest to become someone else, to discard her giftedness, and to don a sanctioned uniform to be accepted. Think about how freeing and welcoming God's grace is. That is what moms long to receive from other Christians.

When I edited *Christian Parenting Today* magazine, I remember reading about the huge number of women who came back to church once they had kids. These women (and probably men, though I remember it as women) had been either estranged from or bored by church, or perhaps had simply never been churchgoers. But once they had kids, they felt drawn—for one reason or another—to put some church into their kids' lives.

I now worry if these women are finding a gracious reception. If active members of the Body treat certain Christians in a less than accepting way and leave bruised members in their wake, how are visitors being received? If they are asked only about their children and not about the people they are and the individuals God created them to be, how are they experiencing grace? How can they understand what this "knowing you and loving you still" kind of love feels like?

Mind you, I'm not saying we shouldn't minister to the mother in them—and we absolutely *must* minister to the kids—but I can't think of a better expression of grace, of the loving acceptance of our Lord, than to say to these women, "We love who your kids are, and we love who you are. We can't wait to see what God has in store for you. We know that your gifts, your personality, your passions, and your whole self can enhance this community."

This will require a change from slapping I.D.'s on the moms, the men, the kids, the marrieds, the singles, the older folks, and other groups defined by market researchers and grouping them into their own little circles. This might work well for some, but not for all.

I mean, I *need* mom friends who have kids my kids' ages. These moms help me deal with the day-to-day craziness of life—no one can understand like they can! That said, when we look only at the sweeping generalities, we tend to base the pursuit of community on external, even artificial, factors.

As much as I like connecting with fellow, in-the-crazy-trenches moms, I love getting to know other people with whom I share interests. I've been just as blessed and grown just as much from the book clubs (peopled with *all* types of readers), from random conversations in fellowship hall or at church picnics, or from strategizing and planning with CEOs on committees at church. These areas of fellowship—which have nothing to do with motherhood—increase my sense of connectedness and allow me to use my other gifts.

In fact, imagine what our church communities could look like if we paid attention to our differences, celebrated each person's uniqueness; if we were gracious hosts, anticipating the needs of family, friends, and guests alike; if we knew what made one another tick, what touched our hearts, what lit our fires? We could connect with people within our congregations or broader communities—beyond just our outward, obvious roles—in innumerable ways. Imagine the strength of that bond if we were connected in many different ways. Imagine what we could do for God's kingdom if, instead of enforcing fake conformity, we inspired and equipped each other to live to our fullest capacity, to our God-given potential—to meet needs and reach people.

What would happen if Bible teachers and preachers and others stopped telling moms who struggle with who they are simply to "find their identities in Christ"? What would it look like if we stopped giving pat answers (even when they do sound biblical) and instead asked good questions and then really listened to each other? In a world where people struggle to fit in, where no one measures up, where fake I.D.'s and unreal expectations abound, what if church were the one place moms could come to find love and acceptance and value and encouragement and *grace*? What if church were the one place where moms felt *totally* welcome and at home?

I think we'd find the church God intended. And it can all start with you.

QUESTIONS FOR REFLECTION AND DISCUSSION

- Do you think it's fair to blame us women—as the church—for our role in passing out fake I.D.'s? Why or why not?

- When you are at church, do you encounter more or fewer stereotypes and assumptions than those who are not moms about who and what you are?

- Have you ever felt like a fish out of water at your own church? If so, what do you think contributed to that? If not, what kept it at bay?

- When have you experienced the grace of being welcomed as the person you were made to be? How did that make you feel?

- At the end of the chapter, this question is raised: "What would it look like if we stopped giving pat answers (even when they do sound biblical) and instead asked good questions and then really listened to each other?" What do you think it would look like?

PART 2

The Seven Secrets to Finding Your Real I.D.

CHAPTER 6

Secret #1:
Get Over the Guilt

It's time to reject the burden
you don't deserve

When Henrik was probably three, he lost his cartoon privileges for the day for some misdeed committed on our way to preschool. (I like to think it's because I'm a good mom that I forget what exactly he did wrong!) As we headed down the back steps toward the garage, he complained on and on about the harshness of the punishment, about it not being fair—you know the drill. When I told him it didn't matter whether he thought it was fair, since the decision was final, he stopped in his tracks, turned toward me, and said with a mean little face, "You're a *bad* mommy. And you're doing the *meanest* thing ever."

Bad mommy, huh? The funny thing about this is that I had told myself that very thing—quite convincingly—probably a million times in the three or so years since I'd been a mom. And yet, as those same words shot out of my son's pinched, yet still cute, little mouth, I knew they weren't true. I was—by standing my ground, by setting limits, by establishing consequences—doing a *good* mommy thing.

The moment stands out for me not because it made me feel bad, mad, or even sad, but because I realized then how big a role guilt played in my life as a mom. When Henrik told me I was "bad" and doing the "meanest thing," I was confident that he was wrong. So why did I so easily accept the misguided but guilt-inducing things that others told me?

Guilt is as hot a topic for the mom set as identities are. We moms feel guilty for the strangest things—and place blame on ourselves for just about everything. If we plan a picnic and it rains; if our daughter's soccer team loses the big game; if too many kids fail to show up for our son's birthday party—somehow we're quick to take the blame. Guilt seems to be built into us—and certainly shoved upon us.

Stephen Colbert offers this bit of his "truthiness": "For a mom to be happy, every moment away from her children must be filled with the soul-wrenching thought, 'Am I a bad mother?'"[1]

If you're not familiar with Mr. Colbert, he's a *satirist*, so don't take his observation seriously. However, I find this, as Homer Simpson would say, "funny because it's true!" Or almost true. I don't actually think I find happiness in asking myself if I'm a bad mother, but there is something about our guilt—and wondering if we are, in fact, good moms—that seems part and parcel of the whole image of the good mom. Like, a good mom should feel guilty if she's not always kid-centered. She should feel guilty when she enjoys time away from her kids (or entire family). She should feel guilty when she longs to—oh I don't know—be seen, known, and loved as her real self.

Of course, this is the kind of guilt we need to get over. This is not to say, however, that *all* kinds of guilt are ridiculous. We do often feel guilt for good reason. For example, a mom should feel guilty if she's neglectful or cruel or withholding love from her kids. And moms should feel guilty over "lesser" offenses too. God certainly uses guilt to lead us out of bad behavior and on toward growth. And then there's the little thing that without guilt, there'd be no understanding of grace.

So, where to from here? Because we moms spend and even waste so much time feeling guilty—especially where it pertains to our identities—we need to work on this a bit. At least I do. Truth be told, the whole idea of this book was born out of guilt, of my wanting to explore why I shouldn't feel bad for wanting to be known, for wanting to be loved, valued, and appreciated as *more* than a mom.

I hope that after reading through the first part of this book, you recognize that there's nothing to feel bad about just because you want to uncover your true self from behind all that mom you've got going on. You know that God cares about *his* identity. And that he not only cares about yours but made you on purpose for a purpose that extends beyond motherhood.

That said, the guilt thing runs deep in all of us. One member of the Big Mom Group had this to say about her own struggle: "I feel really disappointed in myself for all kinds of reasons: I don't spend enough time with the kids. I don't get out enough. I'm too controlling. I never play the piano anymore. I could go on and on…!"

Without question, guilt is such a burden that it's useful to take a look at three areas that can help us work through any lingering concerns. And, in fact, I've discovered some areas of my own identity crisis for which my guilt was pretty legit.

Since this is a book on identity, I want to try to tackle the guilt and come closer to owning our true identities in one fell swoop. And I've got a nifty series of three G words that will help us.

In one sentence, here is the first of seven secrets that you need in recovering your true identity: Become known and loved as the real you by getting over the guilt. And to do that, let's look at Gifts, Growth, and Grace.

Your Gifts

When it comes to feeling guilty about our mom I.D.'s, it mostly has to do with how closely we conform to the prevailing, accepted, "sanctioned"

Christian-mom stereotype. If we're fairly close to matching up with the expectation *du jour,* we feel better about ourselves. If for whatever reason that just isn't us, we feel guilty. We think there's something wrong with us. We're quick to believe a false stereotype while overlooking what God says about us.

Out of curiosity, I asked the Big Mom Group what words they feel describe a stereotypical mom—not a perfect mom, not their mom, not them as moms—just a mom. The words they came up with painted a pretty accurate image of the stereotype (is that an oxymoron?). Their answers fell into two main categories, "Positive" and "Negative," so I've broken them down that way. However, I added a third—the "Eye of the Beholder" category—for reasons that may be obvious.

Negative
- too busy to take care of herself
- doesn't have her own money
- works like a "slave"
- doesn't get enough sleep
- carries the weight of the entire family on her shoulders
- once smart, now has "mommy mush" brain
- showers infrequently
- boring
- dull
- old
- settled
- doesn't worry about how she looks because all that matters is the kids
- busy
- tired
- uptight
- out of touch

Positive

- creative with crafts, car-ride activities, and consequences
- forever nurturing
- patient
- consistent
- child focused and home focused
- attentive
- runs home like a good manager
- someone who's happy at home, watching TV and playing with the kids
- nice
- understanding
- loving
- cooks and bakes
- has it together
- wise and knowledgeable
- devoted
- energetic
- pretty
- organized
- good at arranging children's activities
- into volunteering with the PTA
- responsible
- protective
- helpful
- scrapbooks everything perfectly

Eye of the Beholder (you decide if these are positive or negative)

- perfectionist
- always cleaning
- cares about curtains[2]

- conservative
- June Cleaver
- someone who makes sandwiches and cuts them into triangles[3]
- coupon clipper
- minivan driver

When I followed up by asking which of these attributes characterize members of the Big Mom Group, they were heavy on the "Negative" and light on the "Positive" (and sort of in-between on the "Eye of the Beholder" list!).

However, when I asked what their gifts were and how their gifts meshed with mothering, they came alive! Suddenly, it was all positive. No one ended up sounding like the one-dimensional, unimaginative, child-obsessed woman we see portrayed in the stereotype. Everyone sounded like a gifted, loving mother committed to her kids. It was great to see.

Yet all of us, at one time or another, beat ourselves up because we don't match some stereotype—instead of focusing on the gifts God gave us to raise our kids as he wants them raised.

For whatever crazy reason, God chose me to mother the three kids I've got (just like he chose you for your kids—though I'm not implying that I think he's crazy for giving you your kids!). He wanted my children to live in a house with a woman who thrives on writing in the midst of chaos, who isn't all that organized, who gets a charge out of new ideas and collaborating with bright people. Who loves her kids, but isn't very good at many of the typical mom things. Three kids in, I still have no clue how to get a baby to sleep without rocking or nursing, I'm still terrible at setting up play dates, I'm not good with consistent discipline, and I'm prone to yelling when I get frustrated (thank God, I'm quick to apologize!). But for whatever reason, God saw me and the things I'm great at—snuggling, talking, walking, writing, creating, encouraging, loving, forgiving, recognizing teaching moments—and decided Henrik, Greta, and Fredrik were the right ones for me. Go figure. I'm one blessed

things good at
things not good at

woman. Seriously, no offense, but he gave me the best kids. They are by far my best gifts.

When moms spend time feeling guilty because our gifts don't line up with how others say a mom should be, that's false guilt—straight from the Enemy. He is the one who wants us to flounder and ultimately fail in the world of fake I.D.'s, rather than shine in the realm of true, God-given identities.

Your Growth

The thing about guilt is that sometimes it's not false or undeserved. At times it is, indeed, "true"—and quite handy. You know the saying "Just because you're paranoid doesn't mean they're not out to get you." Well, with guilt, just because you feel guilty too much doesn't mean you're never doing anything wrong.

No question, God gave us guilt to turn us away from wrong and point us in the right direction. Never feeling guilt would be sort of like the people who, because of a physical malady, don't feel pain. It doesn't sound so bad until you realize what would happen if your hand were resting on a hot burner and you couldn't feel it. Guilt is like that. While it hurts like the dickens, if you're paying attention and have good reflexes, feeling the burn or the guilt can save you—or at least your hand.

In the same way that pain can lead to growth (as in, being wiser about where you put that hand in the future!), so can guilt. Being in tune with our guilt allows us to grow as God wants us to—in all areas of our lives. But when it comes to our identities, I think the guilt sensors tend to go off for a couple of different reasons: One, when we moms do lack some important things mentioned on the lists from earlier in this chapter. And two, when our concern with our identities *is* selfish, having more to do with ego (as one woman kindly pointed out to me once) than with being known. We'll get to that one in a minute. First, back to the lists.

While the "Positive" or even the "Eye of the Beholder" lists contain some things that may be unattainable or simply outside our gift ranges, there's plenty there that we *should* be going for. Many of these come naturally to us. Perhaps the traits of being loving, protective, devoted, helpful. But what about some of the others? What about nice, attentive, patient, consistent?

Speaking for myself, of course, I see that these are areas I can grow in. Take "nice": while I normally am a kindhearted mother, catch me on the wrong side of five hours of *in*terrupted sleep and I get mean. When I'm aggravated and snapping at others, I must sound awful to little ears. Same with attentive, patient, and consistent: I don't think it's unreasonable to expect a mom (or anyone!) to be these things, but the reality of our lives makes them difficult to pull off on a regular basis. Right now I'm writing in a quiet room, but this is not the norm. Just like you, I'm sure, I spend most of my days juggling twenty things at once, zooming here, jogging there, and this leaves little space for proper attention, patience, or consistency.

But it isn't a good excuse. The guilt I feel when I'm mean, not paying attention, impatient, or inconsistent stings for good reason. I need to grow. I need to do better. As a mom and, of course, as a complete woman. These need to become part of my true identity.

Then there's the second area where we need to grow a bit: when the reason we struggle with our identities has more to do with selfishness than it does with wanting to live as God made us. For example, I'd like people to know me as a writer and a mom. Mostly, it's important that others know me as a writer because then they'll know a bit about how I process my life, make sense of things, how I see the world, what I love to do, and maybe why my house is, as one friend says, "artfully messy."

And yet, there's another reason I want people to know I write. It can be summed up in two words: James Schaap. Allow me to explain. When I was a senior in high school, a respected and talented writer and college professor came to my school to lead a writing workshop. While he was there, he judged our annual Fine Arts Festival.

And that's when he dissed my short story. Totally. As chair of the Fine Arts Committee, as a good writer (really—you can ask my teachers) in my small school, as a girl with dreams of being an *author*, that competition was mine to *lose*—and I did. Thanks to James Schaap. So, seriously, every time I've ever published a story or done anything relatively cool or "admirable" in the world of publishing, my brain goes back to being a seventeen-year-old loser and I think, *What do you have to say now, Professor Schaap?*[4]

As you can see, this is a problem. That part of wanting to be known—of perhaps hoping that Professor Schaap somehow gets wind that the girl he passed over in 1990 became a published author—is admittedly selfish, completely immature, and something I need to get beyond.

While my case is extreme—and a bit psycho—you might have similar issues that you struggle with. One of my friends likes to take her kids and a satchel full of work to a neighborhood coffee shop. That way people can see her with her huge bag of books and files—and know that she, indeed, has a more interesting life than "just a mom." Her desire to be known more fully is legitimate, but I also understand why she'd feel selfish about it. Why does she need to project an "image" for people she doesn't even know?

The solution for all of us starts with prayer. If there's one thing I've realized about God in thirty-some years of praying, it's that while I may get a lot of no-go's and my share of silence, whenever I've prayed for growth, for help and strength to become more *like* God—more loving, more attentive, more patient, less selfish—it's a definite go! In abundance. And you'll be amazed at the ways he works this out to get you growing.

The other thing is to take a guilt test—and don't cheat. In her book *Motherhood: The Guilt That Keeps on Giving*, Julie Ann Barnhill borrows a bit from Mary Whelchel (no, she's not the one who was Blair on *Facts of Life...*) in coming up with a good way to determine true guilt from false. Julie suggests you ask: "Do I know why I'm feeling guilty for this particular thing, and do I know what I'm supposed to do about it? If the answer is yes, then you are dealing with true guilt. You can actively pursue the 'supposed to do about it' part and move away from its power to weigh you down as a mother."[5] Don't you love that? It's advice that is at once empowering and opens the doors to grace, which we'll move on to now.

Receiving Grace

Back when I edited *Christian Parenting Today* magazine, a woman pitched an idea for an article about the regrets of motherhood. One of her biggest regrets, she wrote, was that she never hugged her kids or even *once* told them she loved them. She had thought her acts of taking care of them, cooking for them, and doing their laundry would have spoken of her love for them. But now that they were grown (and probably in therapy and not speaking to her), she realized she had probably made a mistake in never actually saying "I love you" to her kids.

Ya think?

While I like to think the mistakes I've made as a mother (and I've made a bundle) aren't quite as bad as withholding hugs and not telling my kids I love them, I still have plenty of serious regrets. Things I can't undo. Things I wish weren't part of who I am.

A few page flips later in that same fun book on guilt (yes, there really is such a thing), Julie Ann Barnhill writes this: "So if you feel as if you've failed or screwed up as a mom—well, chances are you probably have."[6] Well of course. As moms, as wives, as daughters, as athletes, as musicians, as artists, as humans, we *screw up*. Royally. Again and again.

This would be a lot more depressing if it weren't for a simple—yet amazing—thing. Grace. Here I go again. You can probably tell I'm a bit grace-obsessed. I credit that to my Calvinist upbringing and continued immersion in the Reformed tradition. We Calvinists love our sin—well, talking about it, I mean. If talking about mistakes and past sins bums you out, it's because you're missing the point. You need to talk about sin and guilt to understand grace and the *depth* of God's love for us. And there's no way, I don't think, you can be bummed once you really *get it* that God loves you *so much* that he sent his Son as a sacrifice, to pay the price, as we say, for the bad things you and I have done.

No matter what we've done as moms or otherwise, when we accept the gift of God's grace in the death and resurrection of his Son, Jesus, God tells us, "Sure. You messed up. Sure, you're still going to mess up. But you know what? I love you—I think you rock! And I took care of that sin. Slate's wiped clean. You can move on, and I'll move on with you."

Accepting this grace is not only good news for the life that awaits us after death; it's also good news for life on this planet, for the here and now.

As Julie Ann Barnhill says, grace allows us to "unburden" ourselves, to live freely, fearlessly, and hopefully, knowing that we will mess up again and again and it'll be okay. We'll be forgiven and have a chance to learn from those mistakes. That unburdening allows us to focus on the work God created us to do—here. It allows us to focus on the lives we were made to touch and the needs we are to meet, and to do all these things without oppressive guilt. Instead, we can be confident in who we are.

After that grace fix, what to do? If you can believe that God made you on purpose, for a purpose, that he cares about you as you are—as he made you—and that he can help you grow into more of who you are made to be—a fuller, freer version of you—it's time to take care of the guilt. Look at the areas of your life where you feel guilty, and put them through a couple of tests. First, ask yourself the true-guilt-versus-false-guilt question: do you indeed know why you feel guilty and what you are supposed to do about it, as Julie Ann Barnhill writes? If yes, then do that. You can ask God to forgive you (and accept his grace) and to help you learn from your mistakes and grow from them.

If you can't pinpoint why you *feel* guilty, then it's probably your fake I.D. wreaking havoc with your life. Most likely, you feel bad because you're not gifted in an area in which you *think* you ought to be gifted. Like my wishing sometimes that I were a perfect hostess. You can go to God with that too—ask him for that "gift." If he gives it to you, great. Who doesn't like more gifts? If not, great too. Be reassured that you are who you are for a purpose. There is no guilt in living out the life God created for you, being who he made you, and using the gifts he gave you—even when they don't match up to the accepted stereotype.

That's freedom from guilt. That's grace.

QUESTIONS FOR REFLECTION AND DISCUSSION

- Without looking at the list of assumptions about the perfect mom, in which areas do you struggle with guilt?
- Look again at the list of positive motherhood traits. Which of these are strengths that you have?
- How are the gifts that God gave you put to good use in your life as a mother?
- How often do you beat yourself up because your gifts don't match up with others' ideas of what a good mom is? What's the outcome of that?
- Have you accepted the grace that Jesus offers? If not, why? Would you like to?[7]
- Can you believe that God made you on purpose, for a purpose, that he cares about you as you are—and that he can help you grow into more of who you are made to be?

CHAPTER 7

Secret #2: Find Your Identity in Christ

It's the right answer, but sometimes it's misunderstood

If you move in any Christian circles and have wrestled at all with your identity, I can almost guarantee that you've heard this: "Find your identity in Christ." Usually you hear it at the end of a discussion—maybe in a Bible study group or a breakout group during a women's retreat. And usually, after the words are uttered, if you look around, you'll see smiling faces nodding in agreement.

But how many of the nodding women are nodding just to fit in? I've got to tell you, until recently I might have been smiling and nodding along too. But in my head I was going, *WHAT?!?!*

I've long considered this "find your identity in Christ" business to be largely a brush-off. It has become a convenient pat answer to silence the moms who are struggling with their identities. And at best it's a good answer to the wrong question. Let me explain.

I sense the brush-off when someone doesn't want to open things up for an honest discussion about our identities. Perhaps they don't want to face why we moms might be feeling like this, or maybe they're afraid that such a discussion would cause them to reflect on their own identities.

(Some of the most conventional, full-throttle moms I know are the ones who protest a little too much, if you know what I mean.) It is, frankly, hard to argue with an answer that ends with the words "in Christ"— especially when the answer is given with that kindly, reassuring hand on the forearm. I mean, who's going to question that?

The good-answer/wrong-question aspect comes into play when we hear we are to find our identities in Christ as it applies to our *worth as people.* Moms have good reason to struggle with lack of confidence, low self-esteem, fatigue, and all the other things that tear us down. If you struggle to feel like you're worth something as a human being—or as a mom—knowing that you are *anything* in Christ sounds pretty awesome, right? And then you add on the reassuring hand-on-the-forearm gesture, and you're over the moon!

I was reminded of this one morning while flipping through television channels. I caught the end of a Christian program as they pitched a new DVD from a prominent Bible teacher. The DVD was called "Knowing Who You Are in Christ," which caught my attention. But the promo pitch that followed tapped in to the whole self-esteem thing. The commercial showed desperate-looking people saying things like "I am nothing..."

I don't mean to diminish that real need we all have to know we are something. And I would never diminish the pain that comes with feeling unloved and worthless. But these struggles are not the same as the deep desire to know *who we are.* Self-esteem and personal identity are two very different things. I can feel that I'm worthy of being known and still be convinced that I am completely unknown. See the difference?

So I think that when we begin to wonder just who we are now that we're moms, it's less about worth (because Christians have done a *great* job of giving the "mom role" a lot of good press!) and more about self. That's why the "find your identity in Christ" answer doesn't always fit. If you are a Christian, you *know* that you belong to Jesus. You *know* you're "redeemed by the blood of the Lamb" and that God loves you more than you love yourself. You *know* you're a new creation in Christ. But those same things can be said about—no offense—*any* Christian. This could be a man, for crying out loud. And he will never be a mother. Not even close.

So for a Bible study leader or retreat speaker or pastor or Christian television personality to tell moms that they find out who they are by finding their identities in Christ is like telling moms they're essentially identical to a grandfather, a teenage boy, a career bachelor, a dad with eight kids, a Wall Street power broker who is divorced and hasn't seen his kids in six months, a newborn baby—you get the idea. It assigns moms to the generic batch of humanity. Yes, God loves moms desperately. But that's not who we are!

The Identity Struggle

When we wrestle with our identities, we want to know who *specifically* we are. Who we were made to be. Why we're gifted the way we are—and how that all fits into our role as mom as well as our lives as women who follow Jesus. So the next time you're given the "find your identity in Christ" answer, smile your acknowledgment but don't nod your head in full agreement. Because you're asking a completely different question.

Or you could probe a bit deeper. I thought about not including this chapter in the book, but the more I talk to other moms, the more this issue keeps coming up. People I love, admire, and respect—my wisest friends—keep talking about it. So does C. S. Lewis, of all people.

So I took another look at the wisdom that has been offered by others, and I liked what I saw. What I've discovered is that the true secret of "finding your identity in Christ" is in its placement in the discussion. It's not the conclusion to the question of where to find your identity. It's the *beginning*.

Do pass go

One of my issues with the find-your-identity-in-Christ line, I think, is that it smacks of a quick and easy answer that fails to address the complexity of the question. I need to tread carefully here to explain what I mean. As a Christian, as a grateful child of God, and as a follower of Jesus, my ultimate identity *is* the part of me that is enlivened by God's Spirit. If all else were stripped away—my children, my husband, my mind, my passions—if I just vegetated in a hospice bed doing nothing, nearly *being* nothing, I'd still be a beloved daughter of Christ (with a purpose). So it's not that I am ashamed of this part of my identity.

In fact, that is the part that's secure. I don't question it or wonder what I'm to do with it. No one has tried to take that part away from me, so it's not something I wrestle with. As I type these words, I realize it's yet another blessing I have as a Christian—the freedom to be and to express this part of my identity. I know that since I am in Christ, "the old has gone, the new has come!" (2 Corinthians 5:17) in terms of how I look at life.

However, when the identity mantra is uttered in certain contexts, from certain people, I do get the sense that when I'm told to find my identity in Christ, I'm being told to do a better job of toeing the party line. I suspect what they actually want me to find is an identity that supports their approach to being a Christian—conforming to the rules and values and terminology of the group.

There is a big difference between supporting the group and following Jesus. (Can I get a quiet "amen"?)

Again, I find nothing wrong with being identified as a Christian. To know me as a born-again Christian in the "Reformed neighborhood," as a friend of mine describes it, is to know a lot about me. You can guess at the ways I've been shaped by my church's roots in a strong, proud, Dutch heritage and culture.

So just as with moms, there's a lot we Christians *do* share in terms of identities. Thinking broadly and doctrinally, we:

- Believe that God sent his Son, Jesus, to live as a human and to die as a sacrifice for our sins.
- Believe in the Trinity: the divine relationship of the Father, Son, and Holy Spirit.
- Believe in the Bible as God's inspired truth.
- Believe God reveals himself through the Bible, through his Son, through the Holy Spirit, through creation, and through God's actions throughout history.
- Believe that the Bible not only tells the story of the redemption of God's people but that it offers ways to live the best life here on earth, from taking care of the "least" among us to telling others the good news about God's grace.
- Think fellowship with other Christians is essential.

Beyond statements of faith and historic creeds, we have customs, traditions, and convictions that guide Christians in different directions on various issues. Based on where someone attends church, you might get an idea how that person might feel about women, gays, abortion, Republicans, the environment, the poor, AIDS, homeschooling, Democrats, immigration, war, taxes, evolution, church-and-state issues, and so forth. I'm writing this chapter in the midst of a presidential election season. I think I'll spit if I have to hear one more news analyst tell me how evangelicals are voting.

I bring this up because Christians are, of course, amazingly diverse people with opposing values and commitments and views on hundreds of issues. But when it comes to being a mom, somehow all Christian moms are expected to fit the *same template.* It's like other Christians were custom-built by God, but all of the moms were stamped from the same mold on the same assembly line.

Having our identities in Christ I.D.'s us as Christians—whether we're male, female, young, old, married or not, parents or childless. But being a person who bears the image of God identifies you and me as unique, one of a kind, different from all others, precious creations of God. And that applies even if you're a mom.

So What Do We Do?

I was relieved to discover I'm not the only one who wrestles with the full meaning of finding our identities in Christ. Barb, a member of my Big Mom Group, wrote this in response to a blog I posted on the topic of pat answers that don't answer the question that was asked.

"Well, yes, of course, I have my identity in Christ, but I've got to figure out how to live out that identity in my life, in my circumstances. There isn't just one way—we aren't all little robots that once we identify with Christ, we all say, do, feel, and think the same. No, God created an infinite variety of people who have their identities in Christ. So how do I live out my identity in Christ? That's the question."[1]

A mom named Siska commented on the same blog post: "I have spent a lot of time recently searching for my identity in the Bible, but I wasn't getting anywhere, until God showed me the following idea, which has been helpful.… I was looking in the Bible to see who a child of God is, but God wanted me to get to know him so that I could act more like him and, more importantly, develop my relationship with him. How I understand the nature of God is how I try to be, act, and find my identity."[2]

See what I mean about the wisdom of other moms?

When I first started posing the question of what it means to find one's identity in Christ, a friend joked back, "Right. How is a twenty-first-century Western, married Christian mother who's busy with three active preschoolers and plunking out stories on her laptop supposed to relate to an unmarried, first-century, male Jewish carpenter who spoke Aramaic—who also happens to be God—and lived in the Middle East in a nation occupied by a foreign power?"

Precisely. It's weird to wrap your head around.

But then my friend followed up with, "Maybe you ought to look at how Jesus identified people—or specifically, women."

That's a good start. But we've done that a bit already—back in chapter 4, the "God" chapter. We know that Jesus valued individual personalities, gifts, and abilities. If we look deeper into Scripture, we see also that he liked some people more than others; he had favorites, called people by name, and knew people's life stories before they could be told. He certainly didn't view us all the same—he saw individuals. So it seems as though he wouldn't want our identities in him to be homogenized—anonymous Christians known collectively as "moms."

Jesus' words fortify these sentiments. In John 12:24–25 he says, "Listen carefully: Unless a grain of wheat is buried in the ground, dead to the world, it is never any more than a grain of wheat. But if it is buried, it sprouts and reproduces itself many times over. In the same way, anyone who holds on to life just as it is destroys that life. But if you let it go, reckless in your love, you'll have it forever, real and eternal" (MSG).

Funny thing, when I first read these words—in this context—I got nervous. *Oh no,* I thought. *He doesn't care about our individual lives or selves after all!* Because when we talk about this verse, about loving our lives versus losing them, as the *New International Version* of the Bible puts it, it seems like pursuing one's unique identity would indeed be for naught. That if we were true Christ-followers, we'd chuck everything that is "us" and keep our eyes—and our identities—just in him, just in being Christians.

Again, my friends come to the rescue with some timely wisdom.

"It might be more helpful to spell out explicitly what it means to 'find one's identity' in Christ," wrote Al, the husband of a member of my Big Mom's Group. "That whatever identities we have (mom, friend, coworker, ministry volunteer, etc.), we live out those identities Christianly. Thus it's the challenge of discerning what it means to be a Christian parent or a Christian spouse or a Christian coworker, with all of the various complexities and multiple competing demands and priorities. "[3]

You'd think Al and my friend Barb had talked this over because Barb wrote, "The answer is found in how God has created me (with certain gifts and talents) and shaped me (through my experiences). My identity in Christ is who I am, but it's how I live out who I am that's the question. And, how I discern God's answer above the din of cultural, community, family, and internal (that little voice in my head) expectations is the challenge."[4]

That's it! Finding our identities in Christ is finding in and from Jesus how he would have us live—as *us.* We look to him to show us how to live with what he gave us. And in doing that properly, it means we let go—not of who we are, but of what *we* think our gifts are all about. It means that if we are living who we are simply for ourselves (or even for our kids or husbands or anyone else), but not for Jesus, we're doing it wrong. And if we're trying to live a certain way so we'll fit in with the prevailing church view of what a mom is and isn't, then again we're being false to who God made us to be.

Finding your identity in Christ is closer to focusing your identity on Christ, staking your identity in Christ, perhaps cloaking it, wrapping it, dipping it in Christ. Right now I'm craving fresh berries, and I keep imagining this identity quest as a strawberry finding its fuller identity in sugar. So it goes for a dip or gets a little sprinkle—still a strawberry but, I say, far better: shiny, sparkling, dazzling with sugar. Delicious.

We turn now from strawberries to someone a bit more urbane (though often silly himself), C. S. Lewis.

Living in the Light

When I last read the chapter "The New Men" from C. S. Lewis's *Mere Christianity,* I was newly married in my early twenties, just establishing my career as a magazine editor. I read the book on the train—where I read scores of books over the four years of my commuter life—to a job I loved and then back home to a life I loved. I lived a dream; the culmination of years of schooling, hard work, and, well, dating came together in a new Caryn Dahlstrand Rivadeneira who knew who she was and lived it well.

So it didn't surprise me when I flipped back to this excellent chapter, essentially on our identities, that I hadn't underlined a thing. While it could've been that I was simply eager to finish the book (it *is* the last chapter), more likely it was because when I first read it, I was simply smiling and nodding along.

Reading it now is like a refreshing dessert! Although Lewis gives a much better illustration than my lame strawberry one to illustrate what it is to find our identities in Christ—and still maintain our uniqueness. He writes about people who have always lived in darkness. Because they don't know better, they might assume they are all identical and that if someone bothered to turn on a light, they'd all reflect it the same way and hence look the same to the outsider. However, pop on a light and *voilà!* "You and I know that the light will in fact bring out, or show up, how different they are," he wrote.[5]

He then goes on to give an excellent salt illustration. While it would be logical (especially to Americans who tend to go a bit heavy on the stuff!) to think that adding salt only makes everything taste salty, those of us who love food and cook a bit (or, okay, just watch a lot of Food Network) know that adding salt—the right amount—brings out the natural flavor of the food to which it's added. If I salt, say, a tomato my neighbor picked out of her garden, I'll get *more* tomato flavor, not less. Salt ourselves with Jesus, and we get *more* us, not less.

You'll have to read this chapter yourself to get Lewis's apology for the imperfect illustration (because, he argues, you can oversalt something, and you can't over-Jesus something—I love this!), but I think this is great. The man knows his stuff!

In fact, if people would use this image when they talk about finding our identities in Christ—like adding salt to our identities or turning on the light of our identities—they'd get more than conformist nods and fake smiles. We'd be talking applause and hallelujahs! Because it's so exciting to discover that Jesus makes us more, not less, of who we are. That he's interested in not only who we were made to be but in bringing out the best in us. Wow. He wants to help us shimmer in his light and burst with the flavor he gave us. It's humbling and uplifting all at once.

Of course, it's no accident that C. S. Lewis chose the salt and light illustrations. Jesus himself calls us to be salt and light to the world.

You've read this passage a million times, I'm sure—it follows the Beatitudes. But here it is from *The Message*:

> Let me tell you why you are here. You're here to be salt-seasoning that brings out the God-flavors of this earth. If you lose your saltiness, how will people taste godliness? You've lost your usefulness and will end up in the garbage.
>
> Here's another way to put it: You're here to be light, bringing out the God-colors in the world. God is not a secret to be kept. We're going public with this, as public as a city on a hill. If I make you light-bearers, you don't think I'm going to hide you under a bucket, do you? I'm putting you on a light stand. Now that I've put you there on a hilltop, on a light stand—shine! Keep open house; be generous with your lives. By opening up to others, you'll prompt people to open up with God, this generous Father in heaven. (Matthew 5:13–16)

Our I.D. in Christ is to live as his light in the world, to add his "seasonings" and his "colors" in the way he seasoned and colored us. And we each have our flavors and our own shades and hues, which this world needs.

When we consider our identities—who we are, how God made us, what gifts we've got—how great is it to rethink all that in terms of the ways we've been seasoned and lit by Jesus? By calling us to be salt and light to the world, Jesus is telling us what it means to find our identities in him, I think. We are to take who we are, add him, and shine in this world—doing what he's put us on this planet to do as moms and beyond—bright in flavor, bright in appearance, bright in us, bright in him.

QUESTIONS FOR REFLECTION AND DISCUSSION

- Think about the times someone has encouraged you to "find your identity in Christ." What has that meant to you?
- Has this oft-given advice comforted you or confused you?
- Describe what it means that your full identity is in Christ?
- How does finding your identity in Christ differ from being I.D.'d as a Christian? How are they similar?
- How does Jesus season your identity with salt and light?

CHAPTER 8

Secret #3:
Find Your True I.D.

Discover who you are in God's eyes

After a conversation about how we find our true identities, a friend suggested I read Joan Anderson's book *A Year by the Sea*. Essentially, it's an entertaining and insightful memoir of a fifty-something woman who, after having spent a life in the "traditional" role of capable housewife and doting, loving mother, finds herself completely lost (identity-wise). That's when she decides to take a year off to rediscover herself.

While I wouldn't necessarily recommend *doing* this, I understood the need to take drastic measures to figure all this out. And, I must confess, while reading her book on some particularly rough and exhausting days as a mom, I struggled with outright jealousy of her quiet—if slightly confused—life by the sea.

During Anderson's year living in the family's rickety cottage on Cape Cod, she had all sorts of interesting experiences that led to her figuring out just what her true identity was. Plus, she happened to have the most serendipitous of all serendipitous encounters I've ever heard of. During a stroll along the shore, she met Mrs. Erik Erikson. Name doesn't ring a bell? It didn't for me either. But it turns out Mrs. Erikson's husband is the guy who coined the phrase "identity crisis."[1] Can you imagine that kind of good fortune? *Having* an identity crisis, retreating to work through it, and then bumping into and befriending the wife of the guy who invented it? Some people, I tell ya…

To tell you the truth, after I read about Anderson's astounding seaside encounter, I started hoping that I'd happen upon some identity genius who'd fill me in on all sorts of secrets. In fact, even as I type *right now* at the Elmhurst Public Library, I'm making eye contact and smiling with everyone who walks by. I just *know* that someone will stop, ask what I'm working on, and go, "You know, my daughter is dating the grandnephew of the guy who coined the phrase…" Or something like that. But, alas, no go.

So, Internet, looks like it's just you and me, baby. Seriously, I guess it is time—eight chapters in—that we spend a few moments talking about what an identity crisis is, and what it means for us to be in one. Then we need to parlay all that into some practical ways to figure out just who we are (if you don't know already) and how we want to be known.

So let me just nod and smile at this last person walking by (nope; still no go), and we can get started.

That's Dr. Identity to You

Reading the story of how Erik Erikson became interested in identities made me smile. As a Swede myself, here I was all excited about this guy who seemed like he was a Viking king, what with his super-Swedish name (and apparently he also had super Swedish looks, though that I did not know). Turns out, the guy was Jewish. His being Jewish isn't what made me smile. What did is that the same assumptions I made about his identity were the very things that got him going on this whole identity crisis idea.

Here was a guy who had grown up with every appearance (the fake

I.D.) of a Scandinavian, probably a Lutheran, but who was, in fact, a Jew. So he grew up feeling like he never fit in—because his outsides didn't match his insides. Sound familiar?

Somewhere along the way he decided to figure out this identity thing once and for all. He came up with some good stuff, including eight stages of development that people go through in which a crisis of identity is likely to occur (this includes the starting-a-family years when, if you don't negotiate the identity issues successfully, you feel isolated).[2]

And he did come up with a pretty comprehensive definition of identity (please forgive him for his gender-exclusive language. Apparently, it hadn't occurred to him that locking women out of the pronoun realm can cause identity crises too!) According to Erikson, *identity* can be characterized as "a subjective sense as well as an observable quality of personal sameness and continuity, paired with some belief in the sameness and continuity of some shared world image. As a quality of unself-conscious living, this can be gloriously obvious in a young person who has found himself as he has found his community. In him we see emerge a unique unification of what is irreversibly given—that is, body type and temperament, giftedness and vulnerability, infantile models and acquired ideals—with the open choices provided in available roles, occupational possibilities, values offered, mentors met, friendships made, and first sexual encounters."[3]

This was not a man whose identity included mastering the pithy—or even succinct—statement. All Merriam-Webster's has to say is (for definition 2a), "the distinguishing character or personality of an individual." But that's so much less colorful and gives us much less of a jumping-off point for what happens when we experience an identity crisis.

From a psychological standpoint, what *is* an identity crisis? Here's how Kendra Van Wagner sets it up: "Are you unsure of your role in life? Do you feel like you don't know the 'real you'? If you answer yes to the previous questions, you may be experiencing an identity crisis."[4]

According to Van Wagner, Erikson believed an identity crisis was "one of the most important conflicts people face in development," and he described one as a "time of intensive analysis and exploration of different ways of looking at oneself."[5]

Okay. So now that we've got some background into what makes an identity and what causes the crisis (as if we didn't know!), let's dive into how we figure out who we are. For starters, consider Erikson's ideas about the "irreversibly given" part of our identities. What is a given about you and me, as women and as moms?

(Quick note, though: we're going to leave the heavy psychological stuff right where we found it, with the experts. For one, I'm not a counselor or psychologist, and I don't dispense mental-health advice. For two, I have no idea what an "infantile model" is, as Erikson speaks of it. And for three, I really don't need to be talking about anyone's first sexual encounters—especially my own! If past sexual experiences are an issue for you, and if it involves any guilt—remember God's grace.)

Moving on!

Who Are You, Anyway?

Among the many wonderful things about life in the twenty-first century is that we have no shortage of ways to discover who we are. I can, right now, click over to Facebook and take the "What Disney Princess Are You?" quiz or fill out the "Which Jane Austin Heroine Are You?" questionnaire. I have friends who love these things.

Over the years, I've been e-vited to take tests to discover what sort of dog I'd be, which Desperate Housewife I am, and what primary color I would be. All are interesting looks into what type of people we are. And the Internet also offers more serious personality tests: Myers Briggs, the Enneagram, what have you. Whichever you like, it's there. And it's fun to do this. (Actually I do recommend taking one of these if you never have. Better, though, to have it administered by an experienced practitioner.)

But do those get at what we're talking about in terms of identity? I don't think so. As much as I might see myself in a description of the Myers-Briggs INTJ (which I am, along with only 1 percent of the population—or so I've been told!), it's not how I long to be known. And unless you are acutely aware of the ins and outs of the sixteen different Myers-Briggs personality types or the nine Enneagram types or you're in a group that is doing a serious study of personalities, it doesn't help anyone if you identify yourself primarily by four letters of the alphabet.

What we're looking for in this journey as moms who long to be known is something more organic, more intimate. Definitely something more personal, anecdotal, spiritual. What we want to know—or to have known about us—are the things that really set us apart, that have been placed in our hearts, minds, bodies, and souls by God to be used and developed for the benefit of others. The things, as we discovered in the last chapter, that are to be seasoned and lit up so they can shine.

So how might we uncover these things about ourselves?

The reporter in me says, *Interview yourself!* Ask yourself the questions you'd ask someone else if you wanted to get to know her on a deeper, more intimate level. Don't know what you'd ask? That's okay. I'm about to offer some suggestions. Many are rooted in Erikson's definition of identity.

In fact, why don't you grab a pen for this short exercise, because I'd like you to answer these questions in a two-pass fashion. In the first pass, write down the very first thing that comes to mind, then move to the next question, again answering with the first thing that comes to mind.

Once you've finished the list, go back to the top and give each question a bit more thought. Then you can see how and if your answers change, why you think that is, and how the two answers to the same question work together to reveal something important about you. I'm purposely keeping the questions vague. Answer them any way you like. No right or wrong answers, of course.

Here we go. It's time to interview yourself.

What gets you jazzed?
First pass:

Second pass:

What recharges you?
First pass:

Second pass:

What moves your heart?
First pass:

Second pass:

What lights a fire in your soul?
First pass:

Second pass:

What gets you out of bed in the morning (besides the kids!)?
    First pass:

    Second pass:

What make you feel most like yourself? In what setting(s) are you
    most "in your element"?
    First pass:

    Second pass:

What makes a day a great day?
    First pass:

    Second pass:

What is most important to you?
    First pass:

Second pass:

What are you naturally good at?
First pass:

Second pass:

What talents do you have?
First pass:

Second pass:

What can you do well that most people can't?
First pass:

Second pass:

In a group or a team setting, what do you bring to the table?
First pass:

Second pass:

What did you want to do or be when you were seven years old?
    First pass:

    Second pass:

What did you like to do when you were ten that you still like to
    do today?
    First pass:

    Second pass:

What were your dreams for the future when you were twenty?
    First pass:

    Second pass:

Which of your dreams have come true?
    First pass:

Second pass:

What are your dreams now?
    First pass:

    Second pass:

What do you pray for?
    First pass:

    Second pass:

What have you endured?
    First pass

    Second pass?

What has been your favorite place to live?
    First pass:

Second pass:

What's your favorite place, period?
    First pass:

    Second pass:

What do others need to know in order to know the "real you"?
    First pass:

    Second pass:

What's something about you that few people know but that you'd like
    to be more widely known?
    First pass:

    Second pass:

What do you most want your kids to know about you?
    First pass:

Second pass:

What is it that you most admire about the people you admire?
　　First pass:

　　Second pass:

What do you wish you could strip away to make it easier for others to
　　know you?
　　First pass:

　　Second pass:

What's your favorite form of exercise?
　　First pass:

　　Second pass:

What quality in other people do you value most?
　　First pass:

Second pass:

What gives you peace?
First pass:

Second pass:

What do you feel called to do?
First pass:

Second pass:

So *That's* Who You Are

How'd you do? Were the questions easy or difficult to answer? When I asked my Big Mom Group the question "What does someone need to know about you in order to know the real you?" one of my friends wrote back, "Tough question. How did *you* answer this?"

I hit reply and started plunking away at my keyboard to tell her just what people needed to know to see the real me. And that's when I went blank.

My neighbor Kathryn, however, answered the question on a day when she knew exactly what you and I need to know in order to understand who she is:

> What do others need to know to know the real me? Well, I have
> real, actual goals in life. I have plans! I have hopes and dreams
> of getting paid to bake and to write (even though it may not
> *look* like I am working toward those dreams since my life is
> sucked out of me by my family calendar!). I have a sarcastic,
> quirky sense of humor. I am a helpless romantic. And I want
> a tattoo.

I love her answer. Still, these are tough questions—and they'll be easier to answer on some days than others. (If you're having a hard time, put down the book, get some rest, and come back tomorrow!) Some days, frankly, I have no trouble answering the "need to know" question, but other days it seems all a blur. That's why it's essential to know and have answers to these set in your mind. It's good to have it solid in your heart, mind, and soul. During the crazy times when you have no idea where to even start, it's easy to lose sight of who you are, who God made you to be.

Back to the questions: you'll notice that there's nothing to tally here—the answers have no scoring system. While I hope you came away having thought about yourself a bit more, ultimately, who you are is up to you and God. And while how you want to be identified and known can change, either from life stage to life stage or event to event, the core of who you are—as a mom, as a woman, in Christ—doesn't change.

But adding to the confusion (for us and for others!) is the truth that within that core are seemingly zillions of factors that contribute to our identities, ways we can, in fact, identify ourselves. Think about how these factors contribute to making you who you are: your neighborhood, your family's country of origin, your roles, your talents, your passions, your family, your temperament, your appearance, your image (yes, this *is* different from your looks!), your education level, your job, your kids, your church affiliation, your race, your gender, your language, your income level, your pet preference, your calling. We could go on and on, obviously. There are all sorts of other subsidiary issues that combine to form an identity.

When I was talking to a MOPS group at church earlier this year, one of the women raised her hand and asked, sheepishly, "Is it okay that I think a lot of my identity is in my love of clean countertops? I mean, I really take pride and joy in keeping my kitchen immaculate! It really explains a lot about me."

Of course that's okay! I mean, I *wish* that were my identity. And it illustrates why I think it's so important that we know this stuff about one another. I didn't get the chance to follow up with her, but perhaps the clean-countertop thing would "explain" if she's always running a bit late (had to give them one last swipe) or if she's a total taskmaster with the MOPS clean-up crew. Perhaps asking her more about this would reveal a childhood where her favorite memories were those of her and her grandmother scouring the kitchen. Who knows? But now I wish I had, because these are the tidbits that are *interesting* about a person. And helpful. As I look at my countertops right now, I'm thinking, *I gotta find that woman's number and get her identity going in here...*

Just as knowing about this woman's clean countertops is crucial to knowing her, it's just as important to understand the messy part of my identity. Because the reason my house gets messy in a hurry is not because I'm lazy or that I don't care or because I'm lounging poolside while manservants fan me and feed me grapes. While my brain is good at juggling a lot of other things—writing, editing, snuggling, playing, baking, driving, reading—during the course of one day, the part that is supposed to do all this *and* keep a house organized doesn't work too well. A big part of my identity is that of a woman who can create a magazine article that covers the essentials in just a few hundred words and produces a book (which is tens of thousands of words) out of little more than an idea and a lot of passion. A small part of my identity is that I'm fairly clueless about the best way to organize a room full of toys. Knowing those two things helps you know and understand me. And you would also know that without a doubt, if I did have manservants and could spend my days lounging by a pool, the manservants would not be fanning me: they'd be inside tidying up!

Now, back to you: know who you are yet? If this is still an area you struggle with, you need to spend some serious time praying and reflecting. Ask God to give you a clear sense of who you are, what you're good at, and why he put you where he put you. Ask him to give you a vision for what you were born to do and how he wants you to use it and live it. I believe this is another prayer he'll answer. Because at the end of the day your true I.D. is how *God* sees you and knows you. You might ask what he sees as he shines his light on you.

If answering the list of questions earlier in this chapter was a struggle for you—or if comparing first-pass and second-pass answers to the same questions confused you—spend some time with God as you go through the questions again. Ask him to open your eyes and your understanding to who you are in the many unique facets that make you you. Read a question, talk to God, spend time listening, then write down your insights into yourself.

In appendix A in the back of this book, I've included the list of questions I asked my Big Mom Group. I have worked through these questions, as have more than thirty other women—and the results have been interesting, revealing, and helpful for us as we got to know ourselves and our purposes and desires better.

So, now that we've got a better idea of who we are, let's find a better way to tell the world who we are.

QUESTIONS FOR REFLECTION AND DISCUSSION

- On a scale of 1 to 10, how well do you know yourself?
- In one paragraph, how would you sum up your identity? How do you think this squares with how others see you?
- Which of the "diagnostic" questions from this chapter did you have the most difficult time with? Why do you think that's so? Which of your answers surprised you?
- How does your mom identity mesh with your full identity?
- After working through this chapter, how would you like to be I.D.'d by others?
- Have you asked God to show you how he sees you? If you asked, what did he say?

CHAPTER 9

Secret #4:
Learn to Tell Others
Who You Really Are

Here is a new vocabulary that introduces the real you

Tell me if you can relate: Last Christmas my friend Amy, her husband, and their two young sons attended a party at the hospital where her husband works. As she sat helping her toddler cut his food, a doctor sat down to chat. After commenting on her son's festive sweater, he asked Amy—with a completely straight face—"So, have you ever worked?"

As she continued to cut food, trying to figure out just how to answer this ridiculous question, her son darted off, and she had to get up to chase him. By the time she and her son made it back to their spot, the doctor had moved on—much to Amy's chagrin because by then she had formulated the perfect answer to the moronic question. Thinking back on it, she says, it's just as well the doctor had departed, since her response would not have been appropriate for her child to hear.

I love this story for so many reasons: One, because anything that is this clueless and that offends on so many levels always makes me smile (sorry if that's bad). Two, because it makes you realize (even while writing a book that takes on stereotypes) that sometimes there are good reasons why stereotypes of, say, condescending doctors are widespread. (I mean, honestly!)

But mostly I love the story because it perfectly illustrates what I believe lies at the heart of our identity issues, and that is that we don't deliver the best answers to the thoughtless questions we are constantly asked. We don't have a good vocabulary to talk about our true identities. And without good answers or the right words, we continue to aid and abet the know-it-alls who continue to pin fake I.D.'s on us.

Here's what I mean: aside from the physician's asking Amy "have you ever worked?" we're hit all the time with "so, what do you do with yourself all day?" and "have you ever wished you could have a career?" and "what led you to the decision to put your life on hold so you could raise children?" and "have you always dreamed of being a mom, ever since you were a little girl?" and "what's on daytime TV these days?"

Know what I mean? Here are some of the other things my insightful mom friends have been asked:

- The simple "What do you do?"
- The more complex "So, are you at home or do you work?"
- The ever-offensive "How can you stand it, being with kids all day?"
- Or it's reversed cousin, "Don't you feel guilty, leaving your kids all day?"

Then there are the simple statements people make (meant in love, I'm sure), such as:

- "I love my kids too much to work…" (spoken to a mom who works in an office).
- "I need too much stimulation to be home with my kids all day…" (spoken to an at-home mom).
- And the all-time champion: "It must be nice to have so much time on your hands now that you don't work…" (spoken by a fresh-out-of-college woman to her former boss, turned at-home mom).

I'm sure you could add plenty of ire-inspiring, boneheaded questions to the list. If you've been a mom for any length of time, people have said things that you can't believe you'd ever hear. And as unfair and inaccurate and wrong as they may be, you still can't seem to come up with a great response.

One of my personal favorites involves an exchange between me and my dentist. After Greta (my second) was born, I went in for a routine checkup. Turned out I had two cavities. Same thing had happened after Henrik was born. Up until I became a mom, I had been essentially cavity free—except for one during my lovely braces era. I remember *clearly* my OB telling me that among the weird things pregnancy and nursing and all the hormonal fun that goes along with them can do is make your teeth "weaker" and more prone to decay.

So after the discovery of the additional cavities, I relayed this information to my dentist—to save face, I guess. He looked at me and said, "Well, I don't know about that. I think it's because moms are too busy to brush their teeth. Just another thing they let go."

Okay. The man (a boy, really; he was fresh out of dental school and taking over his dad's practice) said this to me while his fingers were *in my mouth*. Let's just say he's lucky he still has all his digits! While I appreciated his acknowledgment of how busy moms are, "too busy" to brush our teeth? Just another "thing" we let go? What are the other things moms "let go"?

But of course being the polite, nice woman I am (mostly), I said nothing. While I did switch dentists, I've always regretted that I didn't stop him in his foolish talk. I mean, maybe hormones didn't have anything to do with it (if you're a dentist or an OB and would like to chime in, please do!), but I shouldn't have let him create a stereotype and then stick it on me. Still, what *do* you say in a situation like that?

Same thing happened a while back at a writers' group I attend. The topic *du jour* was how to find time to write. The other talented members of the group are mostly working professionals, and if they have kids, they're grown. So while the other writers deliberated on whether taking an hour to write over lunch was better than taking an hour away from television watching at night and grumbled about how to find the right setting and "mood" for writing, I shifted in my seat. The whole time I was thinking, *Try typing with one hand while nursing, people! Try writing a chapter while sitting on the edge of the toilet seat while your kids splash away in the tub! Try writing a sixty-thousand-word book in five-minute increments, constantly being interrupted by someone crying or yelling for you...*

And in the midst of my thought ranting, I heard a writer who was looking in my direction whisper to a colleague: "Must be nice to have all that free time like she does."

I wanted to shout, "Free time? Don't you know I write on the *toilet*?"[1] But, again, I didn't say anything to set the record straight. I want people to like me. And since the false stereotype was *whispered*, I wasn't supposed to have heard it.

But alas, I wish I would've had an answer, a way to dispel that "free time" myth. In fact, I wish we all had answers—ready to fire back at the clueless—that show what our lives are really like, that tell who we really are in clear, easy, natural ways. And you know what? With some thought and some tweaks in the vocabulary we use, we can get there.

Speaking with True Words

Lest you think I'm straying off into psychobabble mumbo jumbo, let me offer this: Romans 10:9–10 says, "If you confess with your mouth, 'Jesus is Lord,' and believe in your heart that God raised him from the dead, you will be saved. For it is with your heart that you believe and are justified, and it is with your mouth that you confess and are saved."

What, you say, has that got to do with setting a blockhead straight? Bear with me for one moment. The apostle Paul is most certainly not talking about our identity crises; he's talking about salvation. But I want to point out the connection between *believing* something and *saying* something. It's more than a linguistic truth; it's a spiritual one. You can believe all you want, but until you "confess" your beliefs, they never become fully realized. I don't think it's at all accidental that Twelve-Step meetings incorporate this technique (i.e., "Hello, my name is ___, and I'm a compulsive gambler").

It makes no difference whether we're talking about belief in Jesus (though this *is* the most important one, of course) or your belief in who you were made to be. It's when you say it that things happen. Saying you believe in Jesus confirms the belief that precedes your words. Saying you believe you have a problem leads you toward recovery. Saying you believe God made you a mom and so much *more* allows you to begin to live your life as God intended it to be lived—and introduces others to the real you.

So let's learn to talk our real-mom walk.

Picking up the lingo

When it comes to moms and identities, you've heard "you're not just a mom" almost as much as you've been told "find your identity in Christ." You know already you're much more than a mom, but yet how many of us have uttered these famous words when asked what we do: "Oh, I'm just a mom."

You're not telling the truth, and you know it. But it's not helpful when the other person says "You're not *just* a mom" and begins a litany of things meant to build you up: "You're a domestic engineer, a baker, a chauffeur, a laundress, a tutor, a cook, a carpool organizer, a coupon clipper, a diaper wiper…" Okay, so maybe nobody ever actually says "diaper wiper," but they might as well. Because this type of litany—which is often accompanied by a reference to the study that claims if what we moms did were a paid profession, we'd make well over one hundred grand—doesn't usually help the mom who says she's "just a mom." We *know* the drill of what we do day after day after day after day… We get the list of duties and know and believe in their importance!

The thing is, I don't believe that moms who answer this way—with the *just* prefix—do it to diminish the role of mother. We don't think moms are lowly, even if other people do. I think we use these words as a cry for help—honestly—and because we have no idea what else to say. The *just* doesn't mean *merely* so much as it means *only,* because, especially if our kids are young and we've put our other gifts on hold, we often feel that's all we're permitted to say we are. Even if we know down deep that we are more than "just" moms—identity-wise—it feels silly laying claim to something outside the mom realm when that, in fact, is our primary role. The language of conventional social exchanges doesn't tend to give moms permission to be more than just a mom.

Same thing goes for the "working moms." I know of moms who wrestle with answering the "what do you do?" question because if they say they are "just" architects or "just" accountants, they feel like they are diminishing the role of mother—like they're segmenting their lives in ways that aren't authentic.

It's all so crazy. Especially as we can be fully moms and fully everything else. The components of our identities aren't so much parts as they are layered wholes. I attribute Shrek and my friend Judy for this wisdom. Shrek, of course, says ogres are like onions—because they have layers, not because they make you cry and smell bad, as his sidekick Donkey guesses.

Judy added to this wisdom when she challenged my then-four-year-old son on his vision for his future. When Judy asked Henrik what he wanted to be when he grew up, he answered, "Half daddy, half chef."

To which Judy said, "Oh, Henrik, don't you know you can be a whole daddy and a whole chef?"

Henrik nodded, but his mommy drifted a second.

You don't say? I thought. And I realized then that while this is something daddies get loud and clear—for the most part—this message does not tend to reach the mommy set. A man can be superdad and the top-producing account executive at Amalgamated Industries for ten years running. But a mom? The assumption is if she's the top producer of anything other than meals, clean laundry, and transportation, she is short-changing her kids.

But we can change that. In fact, we are the only ones who can change that. And we do it by changing the words we use to describe ourselves, the way we use these words, and the manner in which we use them. The good news about this, too, is that it's entirely personal. Just as in the previous chapter, where we concluded that who you are is up to you and God, so goes this thing with language.

While it may not feel like it when we're asked to check the box next to words that "best describe" us or our situations, the truth is, we're not confined to other people's manufactured labels for us. The world does not live and die by the categories of *at-home mom, working mom,* and *alpha mom.* As we discussed earlier, these labels come in handy for marketers and people who organize women's ministry activities. But in real life they aren't useful.

As I say that, I might make two exceptions. In the time I've been researching this topic, I've found a couple of mom labels I rather like, and I mentioned these earlier: mompreneur and hybrid mom.[2] *Mompreneur* is just so fun, exciting, and, well, kind of sexy—and you don't get that kind of charge from most of the "mom" words! And *hybrid mom* cuts to the chase of what we all are—and what we ought to be expressing. While I have yet to introduce myself to anyone as a hybrid mom, it does something so few other labels have done for us. *It begs a question.* Tell someone you are a hybrid mom, and you might, in fact, hear, "Wow, that's fascinating! Tell me more…" (That is, if you don't hear, "What the…?")

But no matter how good the label may be, the real goal is to move beyond labels and get down to our true identities. Nevertheless, a term like *hybrid mom* does give permission for a mom to be a mom and something else, which gets to what I propose we all become and we all say that we are.

A mom and more

In chapter 8 we asked ourselves questions that helped reveal who we really are—on the inside as well as the outside. I hope you came away from that exercise all fired up about who you are. Maybe you have paragraphs written (on paper or in your brain) that tell you (and the world) why God put you here. That would be awesome! If you haven't done that kind of in-depth exploration, I encourage you to do it now.

With that as a start, it's time to do some serious work that will translate who we are into words we can use to reintroduce ourselves to those we come in contact with. I want you to pick one word or phrase from all that you know about yourself—the key, something quick that sums you up the best—and become "a mom and a ___."

"A what and a ___?" you might ask. Glad you did. A "mom and a ___" is one of the best workable answers to the old "what do you do?" question. For many reasons. One, because when you tack your one word or quick phrase onto the end of "I'm a mom and a ___" it gives other people an added point of entry into your life. It gives them a way of getting to know you beyond just the one role. Two, it allows you to be who you are and to be seen and known as both fully mom and fully something else.[3]

There's more. Introducing yourself as a "mom and a ___" does the same thing for you as a good opening line in a story. It's a hook that gets people interested, whets their appetite for more. They automatically want to know more about who you are, what you do, what you love, and so on. It may not capture all of you (and your "mom and a ___" combination may change over time, or from one setting to the next), but it captures much of who you are, allowing for questions and a greater expression of interest in you. It brings your gifts, your passions, and your purposes to the table and brings you out of mom anonymity and into the realm of the known.

It's when people hear who you are and why God put you here that things happen. It's how people know how your gifts can be used, encouraged, strengthened, or maximized when working with others.

Talk about yourself

What is the one thing you'd like people to know about you? (Remember, it doesn't have to be something you *do*!) What's a great point-of-entry word or phrase that captures who you are?

For example, I say, "I'm a mom and a writer" most of the time. Other times, I might say, "I'm a mom and a dog person."

Moms I know say:

- "I'm a mom and a gardener."
- "I'm a mom and an antiwar activist."
- "I'm a mom and a lawyer."
- "I'm a mom and a Christian."
- "I'm a mom and a preschool volunteer."
- "I'm a mom and a runner."

Now it's your turn. Practice saying: "I'm a mom and a ___." Say it with a smile on your face! If it doesn't feel right, pick a different word. Keep trying until saying it *makes* you smile and you feel your eyes brighten. It'll happen.

And, of course, variations on this response abound. You could go more active—something my high school English teachers would like. You could, in fact, "write books and raise kids," "raise kids and raise horses," or "raise kids and keep house," as it were.

The thing is to find the words that work for you, that feel natural coming out of your mouth, but that nevertheless give others a broader picture of what and who a mom is and, more importantly, what and who *you* are.

Opening Up the Word *Mom*

After hearing the story I told of the man who called me mama and my thoughts on moms needing a new language, one of my former colleagues pooh-poohed the idea that moms can solve the problem of people being out of touch. "All the self-help in the world isn't going to stop that guy from calling you mama."

I guess, right? I mean, my friend Amy can be a mom and a columnist all she wants, but rude people will still ask rude questions.

Incidentally, I've got a friend (who wishes to remain anonymous— and no, it's not me in disguise!) who came up with what I think is the world's best response to rude questions. It's something she didn't create for moms, but it's perfect for us nonetheless. After studying John 1:38, where Jesus asks two soon-to-be disciples who are following him after hearing John the Baptist point Jesus out as the Lamb of God, "What are you after?" she had an epiphany. Turns out she had been looking for a way to deal with a neighbor who had a penchant for making nosy comments about her house. While Jesus' response in John 1:38 wasn't answering a rude question, that he gave the seekers an opportunity for self-reflection struck my friend as a good "tactic."

"I knew that rather than guessing my neighbor's motive and allowing myself to be annoyed by it, I needed to give her the space to talk," she writes. "Rather than being defensive, or offensive, I must…approach it from a new way. I must find out what she wants."[4]

I think she has keyed in on something profound. When people are rude, stop to think about what's behind their lack of manners. Clearly, every question has an agenda, but if we can respond to it by seeking (without "snarkiness," as my friend wisely goes on to write!) to look deeper into someone else's need, all the better! Leave it to Jesus to come up with something that good.

In the case of the nosy neighbor, it turns out she was just missing the people who *used* to live in that house and was sad that a couple without children would occupy a house that she felt was clearly made for kids. But finding that out opened the door (literally and figuratively) for a good neighbor relationship.

Those who ask thoughtless questions don't always mean to harm us, but I can't help but think there *is* another way our own language can help. I'm not totally convinced my former colleague is right. While I do think in the short term a language revolution for moms will have its greatest impact on ourselves—the way we feel and the way we're seen individually—larger possibilities loom here, people. I mean, aside from making yourself more intriguing, one thing I love about the "mom and a __" concept is the way it opens up with the word *mom,* then broadens its scope, and gives the word a fluid shape instead of rigid limitations.

To get additional reaction to my premise, I e-mailed my college linguistics professor. I told him of my desire to squash the mom labels and open up the word *mom.* The ever-wise Professor William Vande Kopple wrote back immediately, encouraging exploration in this "very interesting" territory. He thought my goal of making *mom* mean more was a "good one" and suggested books that explore the origin and use of labels and other books that shed light on how to redeem or "take back" words and metaphors that have gone astray or fallen into misuse.

This got me thinking that what does need to happen to the word *mom* is a redemption of sorts. Not that it's ever gone through what some words have—when they become actual bad words!—but it has lost its purpose as it has become shorthand that "fully characterizes" a woman who has children. It's a word that is so tied up in stereotypes that it becomes annoying when some strange man calls you mama, because you know he's not simply speaking to your role and your relationships or of the depth of your love, but that he thinks he's got you pegged, all figured out.

So while we may not be able to stop people from calling us mama, we can reclaim—redeem!—the word. That way, when people see us as *mom,* they know we have kids whom we love more than anything, for whom we'd do or give anything. They know that our lives are changed, our hearts stretched. They know that we now know what love really is, that we understand God's heart better, and that empathy has moved from figurative to literal. They'll know so much about us in general but realize they don't know it all, especially in the particulars.

It sounds way too simple to work, but I believe the "mom-and-a __" language—or any variations—will push this change, will open up the word as well as people's minds. Moms committing to share a broader description of who we are and to offer more entry points into our lives, passions, interests, and purposes will do wonders for the word *mom*— while allowing women to have their rightful honored place as well.

In *More Than Serving Tea,* Christie Heller de Leon writes, "As we become more adept at counteracting stereotypes, we actually *become* the positive examples that we long for."[5] I love that!

And although she's writing specifically about the stereotypes for women within the Asian American community, she is onto some serious truths that apply to moms (no matter which ethnicity) as well: "Although it may take years to completely undo the effects of stereotypes, the visibility and voices of prominent Asian American women can shift the general public's assumptions and associations regarding what Asian American women are like. We are talented, creative and influential women from whom all society can learn."[6]

She continues, "As God restores our true names—*daughter, beloved, chosen,* and *leader*—may we use our names and gifts to influence the world around us."[7]

Hear! Hear!

God has given us moms complex identities and a vast language to express them. Let's do as Christie suggests and use our words and names and gifts to change this world—as God intends for us to do.

QUESTIONS FOR REFLECTION AND DISCUSSION

- What's the best entry point into who you are?
- How do you like the idea of the "mom and a __" response? What's helpful about it, and what's not?
- What are some of the rude questions you've been asked? What are some of the most thoughtless things you've been told related to motherhood? How have you responded?
- Have you ever described yourself as "just a mom"? What did you mean by it? What was the other person's response?
- What does it mean to you that you can at once be fully a mom and fully many other things?
- Which mom labels do you like and identify with? Why? Which ones throw you into crisis mode?
- So, you're a mom and a _____?

CHAPTER 10

Secret #5:
Reveal Yourself
Like God Does

He has given you better ways
to introduce yourself

Earlier this year I "volunteered" (to be honest, it's kind of mandatory) to help out in the free-play area of the Little Lambs preschool program my church runs. In between helping six groups of three-, four-, five-, and six-year-olds make Play-Doh pizzas, getting trains set up on the tracks, stopping children from running, and dissuading one child from using the plastic zebra as a weapon, I chatted up one of the other moms.

Paula had recently moved back to the Chicago area from a stint in Pittsburgh where she had worked as an architect until her son was born a few years earlier. Though she was excited to be back near her family, it "killed" her to leave their house in Pittsburgh behind. She had redesigned it herself, and she and her husband had done much of the work themselves.

In fact, she told me, she had convinced her husband that they should rent the property instead of selling it so that—and she teared up as she said this—one day she could bring her son back so he could see what "mommy can do."

I totally got that—tears and all! Paula's story resonated because I too love being able to show my kids what I can do (thankfully as a writer and editor, no major costs are involved in this). On another level, Paula's story is revealing because this is an area in which we reflect the heart of our God, who longs to reveal himself through the works of his hands, along with his names, stories, and relationships.

We're back to our need to remember that it *isn't* selfish or show-offy (to use a word from my fourth-grade days) to long to be known in these ways. In fact, I think it's key; it's part of our nature, our God-given image, to want to show ourselves this way. And I think we *should* do this. So let's take a look at how to reveal ourselves as God does.

Through the Works of Our Hands

While Paula's story is a good one, you certainly don't have to have something as dramatic as a redesigned house to share your creations with your kids or the world. I think this longing is basic to who we are. I mean, our kids do this all the time. How many times a day do you get called— usually from the complete opposite end of the house—by a child wanting to show you what he did? What about after school? At least in my house, the unpacking-the-backpack time is all about showing me what my kids can do. I love it, and my kids love it!

It's exciting to share in each other's acts of creation. Seeing what my kids create gives me insight into who they are almost more than anything else. Watching my daughter use her imagination to create little dramas (okay, so this is more the works of her mind, but she uses her hands!) with her little people, dolls, action figures, and animals shows me her relational mind with remarkable storytelling ability. Seeing my son's school projects, his cooking experiments, or LEGO creations show me his ability to create both by following directions and by using his own creative brain.

And my baby? You should see what he can do when his big sister gives him a marker when Mommy's not looking! But seriously, these moments when we get to see the works of each others' hands are so telling about our personalities and passions—and they should be. Remember that our wonderful God laid his creations out there for us to admire and explore.

So don't be shy about it! No matter what you create—whether it's baked goods, actuarial tables, a well-furnished room with good flow, an interesting lesson plan, or well-mannered kids—let it shine; let it testify to how God made you. When you let others know what you can do, not only do they enjoy it but they get to know you better along the way.

My friend Cassie hangs paintings that she created all around her house. I love this not only because of the beautiful art, but because you can walk around her living room, feel excited for her about her obvious talent, and hear the stories behind the paintings. It's a way to get to know periods of her life and stories of her family. Through those paintings you learn things about her you wouldn't otherwise have known.

Same thing could be said for the woman I mentioned earlier who wondered if it was okay that her identity was reflected off the gleam of her immaculate countertops. For goodness sake, if you create a spick-and-span kitchen with floors and sinks and countertops that shine "like the top of the Chrysler Building"—as the orphans sing in "It's the Hard-Knock Life"—then go ahead and let others see that about your life. Allow them the enjoyment of knowing you better, and even admire this part of who you are.

Of course, this can run dangerously close to boasting and pride—so we do need to be careful. It's possible to talk about ourselves *too* much (says the woman writing a book that contains more "I" than she'd care to count) or become so obnoxious that we expect *everyone* to care about every little thing that we're involved in.

For the most part, though, just about every mom I know is far from boastful and proud of her *own* creations. (Moms are much more likely to boast about their kids, husbands, or things they have accumulated.) When talking about your own creations, think in terms of inviting others into your life. You are given talents so you can share them with the world. It's not to reflect how great you are, but how great is the God who made you.

Through Our Names

Each of us has a name, but beyond the obvious "Hi, I'm ___," how do our names reveal who we are? Well, you don't have a name like Caryn Anne Dahlstrand Rivadeneira and choose *not* to even use Anne—the only easily pronounceable name in the series—and not have name issues. Not the least of which is that my first name is pronounced CAR-in. Not Karen, as perhaps you've thought all along. And this brings with it all sorts of awkward, when-do-you-correct-someone's-pronunciation-without-seeming-like-a-pretentious-snot kinds of moments.

As you might imagine, my name issues go way back. In fact, one of my favorite grade-school memories is roll call on the first day of fifth grade. The year before, I had been the new kid in school and had to go through my usual phonetic, plus history-of-my-name, plus Swedish pronunciation lessons[1] with my teacher. But in fifth grade, it was all done for me. When the teacher called for "Karen Dahlstrom," a choir of ten-year-olds chanted "It's CAR-in Dahl-strAND!" It made me feel wonderful, befriended, and known.[2]

Even if you don't have a "weird," oddly spelled name, or a last name for a first name, or a guy's name, or an exotic name with too many vowels or consonants, there's still something about hearing the sound of your own name and the way it makes you feel—and the way it tells you how another person knows you. Your name—the way you call yourself or the way others do—says a lot about who you are.

To know me as a Dahlstrand tells you quite a bit about me (that is, if you know any other Dahlstrands! Swedes are a charming people—well worth getting to know). As does knowing me as a Rivadeneira tell you a story—namely that I must've married a Spanish guy named Rivadeneira and chose to tack his name onto my own. Beyond that, if, for example, I introduce myself as Mrs. Rivadeneira, you are going to have quite a different impression of me than if I go by Caryn. Same thing if someone *calls* me Mrs. Rivadeneira; I assume either she knows me through my kids or at least as a grownup—or is being polite. If I'm Ms. Rivadeneira, I assume she either doesn't know me at all and is trying not to guess my marital status—or she knows of me well enough to guess that I do prefer *Ms.* to *Mrs.* (I'm new-fashioned that way).

And then there's the whole realm of which last name we use. Legally, I held on to my "maiden" name and let it become one of my middles. There was just too much of me in there to let it go. And yet, now that I am a Rivadeneira—and more accurately, that my kids are Rivadeneiras—I find more and more of my identity revealed in being one of this clan as well.

I *do* turn any time anyone calls the name Karen. And I don't hold it against anyone if she mispronounces my name. But just as it was in fifth grade, when I hear my name—pronounced correctly—I know it's someone who *knows* me, and that always feels good.

But revealing ourselves through our names is, of course, about more than the phonics or prefixes and first names and last. For many of us, our names hold something deeper.

In college I had a friend whose first two names together were Thomas James. Growing up, he was known as Jamie. But on his first day of college in Mississippi, his roommate—upon being introduced—said, "JAMIE? What kind of a man's name is THAT?" My friend Jamie then became my friend Tom.

But I, along with those who knew him as Jamie, never made the switch. He told me one day how much he appreciated that, because when he heard himself called Jamie, it always felt like "home."

Probably because I'm a total homebody, that always hit, well, home with me—the sense that the way we reveal ourselves through our names can show how comfortable or "at home" with people we feel—and they with us. Nicknames and "relationship" names (I'm talking about *mama, mommy, mother, mom, ma* here!), of course, are the perfect example of this.

When we coo "Mama loves you," followed by a quick inhale, and a "Yes, she does," punctuated with that weird clucky noise we do in our sweetest baby-talk voices to our infants, we're revealing ourselves in our names and in our voices. In doing so, we create a sense of "home" and belonging for our kids. It's a way we mark them as ours and let them know we are theirs. We use a name for ourselves—mama or mommy or mom or whatever you're called—that communicates our connection to them. (Of course, my nearly four-year-old, Greta, calls me, for the most part, Caryn. When I ask her why she doesn't like to call me Mommy, she says, "Because Caryn's your *name*." So apparently I didn't do that great of a job on the old connection with her. It's either that or her sweetly rebellious personality coming through, but that's another book!)

The same connection argument could be made for any family nick-names. My kids each have "pet names"—something I'll never publicly reveal, not because they're embarrassing or ridiculous, but because they're private. They are fun and special names we use for the kids that make them feel loved, that reveal something about them and our story as a family. I assume some day my kids will have friends or loved ones that they are so close to that they'll choose to reveal their nicknames. Their family nicknames will be a way for them to become known as they let trusted others in on our family "secret."

There is a close connection between nicknames and family stories. Consider this gem from Julie Clawson, which I recently stumbled upon at the Faith in a Dress blog: "I gave my daughter a strong name. I wanted her identity to include a symbol of a woman who pursued what was right and followed her dreams even when it defied her society's expectations for women. So my daughter carries the name Eowyn after the warrior princess from *The Lord of the Rings*. Despite obstacles, Eowyn [in Tolkien's novel] chose to make a difference for good... To have that choice, to be encouraged to make a difference, and to have that freedom to live fully no matter one's gender is my dream for my daughter as she grows."[3]

Of course, through Julie's own story of how she arrived at her daughter's name, we learn a tremendous story about Julie—what's important to her, what dreams she has for her daughter, what will be a priority in their family's life. And without a doubt as her daughter goes through life, her name—and the story behind it—will reveal her and her family in a meaningful way. This is the sort of knowledge that gets passed through the generations of a family—how a legacy of names reveals the history of a family. What a wonderful way to be known.

Through Our Stories

Moms are good storytellers. I mean, we can spin a yarn about our kids, their teachers, other people's kids (most notably the trouble ones), the neighbors, our girlfriends, our colleagues, our pastors, that rude lady in line at the store... But we have trouble, I've noticed, telling good stories about ourselves—at least the kind that reveal ourselves in meaningful ways. (Well, that's not entirely true. Our stories may reveal us in meaningful ways, but it takes a bit of reading between the lines to see what's there.)

And by telling "stories," I don't mean that we should expect that anyone cares to sit quietly while we yammer on about every area of our lives (though this *is* nice if you ever do get the chance). By meaningful stories, I'm talking about sharing something about *you*—what you love, what you do, what fires you up, what makes you interesting—instead of you in relation to everyone else.

Totally embarrassing case in point: Moments before I was set to talk to my home MOPS group about this very topic, our "mentor mom,"

Judy, came up to me to ask for something "interesting" about myself that she could use in her introduction. Upon catching my totally dazed and confused look, she pressed me more.

"You know, something that makes you different, something no one would guess about you."

My eyes glanced sideways and down as I thought and thought. Here I was, a woman in the middle of writing a *book* about identities, about to give a talk on why these women need to be open and honest about who God made them to be, and I was totally blank as to who I was. Okay, so not exactly about who I was, but about what made me interesting.

So Judy said again, "You know, like I'm the kind of mom who loves to mow the lawn. You got anything like that?"

I didn't, but her saying that made me ask the obvious: "Why do you love to mow the lawn?" She replied that it gave her time to exercise, create a good-looking yard, and that the kids couldn't bother her. She found peace and solace while mowing the lawn.

Wow. Cool.

So while I didn't come up with such a cool answer, I did come up with: "I'm the kind of mom who really enjoys cooking dinner." While it's not entirely *shocking* that a mom would enjoy this, it surprises me—because I've never been all that domestic—that I truly enjoy the challenge and creativity of putting together a good meal. Plus, I confess, it's a good excuse to get the kids down in front of a video in the other room.

But the best part of that interaction was coming away with language I think is terrific, something I think each of us needs to have in the backs of our heads—part of the story of us, ready to be told at a moment's notice. We should each be able to fill in the blank: I'm the kind of mom who _____. And we should be able to fill the blank space in multiple ways. That is one way we tell our stories.

I love this because it's so simple, yet so telling. And, in fact, it's based in some solid wisdom. Or at least, that's what my dad told me.

When I was fresh out of college and beginning in earnest the process of looking for a job, my dad, who had spent a career in human resources, coached me on the art of being a good interviewee. He prepped me for the vague questions interviewers like to ask—such as "Tell me about yourself" (which is so vague, in fact, that it's not even a question)—by having me think through answers in the exact way Judy framed her answer; i.e., "I'm the kind of person who _____."

While you can't expect random people on any given day to walk up and ask you to tell them about yourself, you ought to have these stories milling around in your brain. You never know when you'll get a moment to share something fun, profound, or interesting about yourself—and you'll never know how God might use that.

Speaking of that, another angle to the whole revealing-yourself-through-stories bit is this: just as God reveals himself through the story of redeeming his people, having an answer to how God redeemed you is something that you definitely need to have handy. I'm not talking about standing on street corners holding a Repent or Burn! sign. I'm referring to the stories of your encounters with God, with his mercy and love. These are stories the world needs to hear.

In an article in *Christianity Today*, famed *Blue Like Jazz* author Donald Miller says, "The chief role of a Christian is to tell a better story."[4] Totally. We'll get to more on why and how we can—and should—do this in a later chapter, but we need to look at our roles as Christians, as people, as moms and see our own stories in them—and see how God wants those stories to be revealed. And just as God used the people throughout Scripture to tell his story, he's using us and our stories to tell his story.

So think through it, and go tell it.

Through Our Relationships

After all these chapters on becoming known for who you are apart from your role in a family, we get to the part where we get to be known better for our relationships. I'm excited. You know why? Because I love being a mom, and my momness tells a lot about me. Same goes for my relationships in other areas of life—to know me as a wife, daughter, sister, friend, neighbor, or aunt is to know some pretty substantial parts of me through which some pretty important aspects of who God made me to be are revealed.

But it's not only because of that. Our relationships can offer a quick access point, if you will, as to how we can relate to one another. In the Christian Reformed church community in which I was raised, we have a game called Dutch Bingo. It's not a real game, of course, but a thing that Dutch people do (and possibly others, though I haven't seen it) to establish who your family is, how you are related to so-and-so, and just in general figuring out how you fit in. It's similar to the game Six Degrees of Kevin Bacon, in which movie buffs can connect virtually any actor, producer, director, screenwriter, gaffer, best boy, or key grip to Kevin Bacon within six or fewer steps—even if that person has never worked on a movie that Bacon appeared in.

Instead of trying to exclude you, Dutch Bingo is meant to get to know you based on your relationships within the community. Simple as that. Likewise, getting to know someone else through her connections often involves learning about her relationships. It's easy to identify with someone who loves her kids like crazy.

Consider this story: A couple of weeks ago I was reading something Bob Geldof (you know, "We Are the World"? At least, that's how I know him!) had written for *Time* magazine about his travels with President George W. Bush to Africa. The story about the incredible work these two were doing on behalf of AIDS victims interested me on many levels. These two men, from vastly different political and world views, came together on an issue as important as AIDS. (Didn't realize "W" did anything about the AIDS crisis in Africa? Maybe that's why Geldof told the president of the United States that he needed better marketers because nobody else knew either!)

But as much as I was interested in the piece, I didn't relate to it. I was reading about a "rock star" (for lack of a better term) and a president flying together on Air Force One doing high-level work, raising high-level amounts of awareness, and in general living the kind of life I will most probably never live—or understand.

And yet, when I got to the part where Geldof asked the president if he had any more Air Force One napkins or doodads of some sort to bring home for his kids, I related—and I got to know this man in a real way. Same with the president for that matter—when he asked the steward to get some special souvenirs for the Geldof kids. These men were acting as *fathers* who loved their kids and knew what a thrill it was when Dad comes home from a trip and brings back trinkets. And in reading about that moment, I *got* these two men. I felt connected—a kinship to them based on hearing about their relationships. Now when I think back to this rock star and the president, I smile—because I understand very well how an essential part of them works.

I think, frankly, this is why groups like MOPS and Hearts at Home and other mom organizations work so well. Because they provide places we can come to and be instantly understood on an important level. It's why one friend of mine still claims that she never felt better understood or truly known than she did when she attended a weekly breast-feeding class at her local hospital. The women who came to that group week after week—essentially to sit around, lift their shirts, and nurse—bonded with an ease she hadn't experienced before, and hasn't since.

My friend still meets with these women because their relationships have gone beyond nursing and mothering. Mostly this happened because of their initial connection; and relatability opened the way for them to be more real about other areas of their lives.

Having the insta-connecting bond of revealing ourselves through our relationships opens doors and lays a foundation for knowing one another in other ways, not the least of which is through our specific relationships. I allow others to see me and know me as the daughter of Harold and Cathy Dahlstrand, the sister of John, the wife of Rafi, the mother of Henrik, Greta, and Fredrik, and so on. Those who know me as being part of specific relationships gain a depth of understanding into my temperament, my situation, my energy levels in ways that might otherwise not be so apparent.

I believe it is through our relationships that we are most able (and intended) to share God's love and grace. It is by seeing me in action with those I love and have relationships with that you might see this area of my life—both the good and bad.

So go out there and let yourself be known. In fact, be proactive and *make* yourself known more fully through your creative acts, your names, your stories, and your relationships. Don't hold back. You were made to be known, and when you are, you are also making your Creator known among those who need to know him.

QUESTIONS FOR REFLECTION AND DISCUSSION

- How might you reveal your identity through the works of your hands? What sorts of things do you create that reveal an important aspect of who you are?
- What does your name—or any of your nicknames—reveal about you?
- What would you tell someone if they asked to hear something interesting about you?
- Fill in this statement: I'm the kind of mom who _____.
- What's your redemption story?
- What do your relationships say about you? Which relationships are the most telling?

CHAPTER 11

Secret #6:
Treasure Your
Limitations

How to love the life you're living

Years ago, I had lunch with a colleague who, during the course of our conversation, described herself as a "total horse girl." I remember this conversation vividly because I am a total wannabe horse girl. As it turned out, my lunch mate basically had the childhood I dreamed of as a girl (the one I still dream of, actually). She grew up on a farm surrounded by cows, sheep, her own pony—and later her own horse—dogs, barn cats, and hundreds of acres of land. She showed horses and apparently still has a room back at the farm full of ribbons and trophies to attest to her horse-girl accomplishments.

As it turned out, however, this horse girl hadn't been on a horse in years. Her father sold her horse after she moved away, and the cost of keeping a horse in the suburbs of Chicago proved prohibitive. Trail rides bored her, so she didn't really do those either. Plus, working and going to grad school gobbled up her time. Didn't sound like much of a horse girl to me. But when I kidded her about this, she looked at me like I was crazy.

"You don't have to be on horseback to be a horse girl," she joked.

She had a point. One I didn't really think much more about until last year, after I read a comment posted in response to "Identity Crisis"—the article I wrote for the Gifted for Leadership blog. Rosalie, the commenter, wrote something that reshaped the way I saw, felt, and thought about this entire identity issue. This might have occurred earlier, when I heard Horse Girl's words. But since I wasn't wrestling with an identity crisis back then, I have to credit Rosalie with giving me some much-needed wisdom and guidance. She helped me land on a way to view some frustrations and "boundary issues" with motherhood in a new way, from a godly perspective.

Rosalie wrote, "I look at it this way: [We need to] keep casting our nets out there, seeking to find ways our gifts can be used that [are] fulfilling. I feel God hems us in at times for his own purposes. He uses our children and their needs to hem us in; he uses our husbands' conflicting schedules; he uses job application rejection. I just pray that I fulfill what it is he wants me to do within the hedge he has erected, and I pray that some day he will free me for more personal fulfillment beyond the precious role of mother."[1]

I can't tell you how often—how many times a day, really—her words "hems us in for his own purposes" bump around in my head. Because motherhood, with all its joys, pleasures, and privileges, does often keep us from doing and living as we think we could, even should, be.

Let's face it: even after we figure out our true identities, come up with new ways to express our identities, and learn to reveal ourselves as God does, we still face limitations that non-moms don't have to contend with. Because young lives depend on us for love, nurture, and their very survival, sooner or later we're going to hit a wall. Or, as Rosalie calls it, a hedge—one that God has put up for his purposes.

That hedge will keep us from living our identities in all areas at all times. I can honestly say that even on my best days as a mom—when we're all having fun, when the kids aren't fighting or whining, and when

I don't feel like I'm messing up anyone's life too much—I find myself brushing up against this hedge, kind of wistfully peering over what's hemming me in. On bad days, I confess, I often feel like mowing right through it!

So what are we supposed to do with this? Is that just a tough break? I don't think so.

Here's where I get back to Horse Girl. No longer living on a farm and not able to board a horse in the suburbs, she was not only hemmed in, but cut off. And yet she described herself—identified herself—the same way she would have fifteen years earlier. Horse Girl understood that who she was didn't depend on where she stood in relation to the hedges that had altered her life. She still knew who she was. I'm sure she hopes for a day in the future when she'll be back in the saddle, but as far as who she was, it didn't change.

I think Horse Girl understood a couple of important things about handling hemmed-in stages of life: One, we need to believe in who God made us to be, in our true identities, whether we're "living" or "doing" them in a big way right at the moment or even in the current year or decade. Two, we've got to become content with our situations.

In the mix of those two things, we need to remember that our identities never lie dormant even when it seems like they're lying pretty low—like when your dad sells your beloved horse. Instead, we've got to keep looking to God, casting those nets, as Rosalie wrote, in every instance of our lives—whether hemmed in or roaming free—to see how God wants us to use our present life to grow, to develop, to love, and to become more of the women he made us to be.

Claim Your New Expectations

For the second year (that I've known about, at least), Denmark has ranked highest in some "Happiest Country in the World" competition.

Maybe it's not a competition so much as a study, but either way, according to a group of researchers, the Danes are the happiest people on earth—and not because they're blond, beautiful, eat tons of pastries, or have that great mermaid statue at the harbor. No, they are the happiest because—get this—they have low expectations.

When I first read about this last year, it floored me. I've always been a sort of high-expectations kind of girl myself and thought of myself as reasonably happy—especially when I met those expectations!

But since reading about the Danes, I have experienced all sorts of times when going into situations with high (actually, *unrealistic* is more like it) expectations caused unhappiness or disappointment. On the flip side, I've had times when I've purposely lowered my expectations to find—surprise, surprise— it *does* yield considerable happiness. It's the "nowhere to go but up" and "everything else is gravy" philosophies at work.

Not that I think happiness should be the meaning of life and everything we strive for, but this low-expectation idea does have some relevance when it comes to our identities—particularly as mothers who are feeling hemmed in. Follow me here: sometimes I think our identity issues (i.e., our unhappiness with the fake I.D.'s we've been given) have less to do with who we are or how we're gifted and more to do with what we think we should be doing (*ahem,* achieving) or how we *should* be living.

I can't help but think our high-expectation, can-do culture has something to do with this. Society tells us what we do is who we are, so that we are given fake I.D.'s not just as moms but in every area of life. The trouble comes when we accept the fake I.D.'s as being valid and get frustrated at the temporary hedges that God puts in place. We fail to trust him, to trust that he knows what he's doing and that he knows us better than we know ourselves. I mean, he *is* the One who made us on purpose with purpose.

Consider these two stories that have nothing to do with moms but everything to do with identities and their influence. Blair Anderson, a contributor to the Gifted for Leadership blog and founder of avisual planet.com, wrote a post about a man in her neighborhood whom she calls Waving Man. She knows little about him except that he is perhaps in his thirties and that, from certain aspects of his demeanor, she guesses he has a lower-than-average I.Q. But most notably, she knows that he stands out in front of his house on a busy street and waves—all day, every day—at cars going by.

After writing about the incredibly positive effect his waving had on her and her neighbors (as well as the effect of waving back!), she ends her post with, "Maybe it is only the simple repetition, but profound things can be simple too. Was God's divine assignment for this man to wave? Of all the things that our society would hope for a person—accomplishment, success, or at the very least a clean shirt—this man gets to wave. But there is something in his wave that challenges the constant drone of the daily demands that we place on ourselves. Does the uniqueness of that act alone make it some sort of cosmic conduit that connects us to God because we are forced to reflect? Like a life preserver thrown out in a sea of hurry, stress, ambition, and guilt to allow us to grab hold of a moment that is peaceful, transcend the chaos, Waving Man waves.

"I think it is interesting that every time I see Waving Man, I think of Jesus."[2]

A comment from JoHannah heightens the impact of this post for me. She writes: "I love your thought that God's divine assignment for this man is to wave. I have a good friend whose son is severely disabled, but he loves to smile. She calls him her 'happy boy' and says it lifts her spirits to see him (mine too). It's great to think that God created him to smile."[3]

So here we have two dazzling examples of people hemmed in—by mental or physical disability or by circumstance—with hedges higher than we'll probably ever experience, and yet they excel at living out who they are. It's easy for us high-expectation, overachiever types to think our identities have to be lived large, all the time, to qualify as respectable identities. It's hard for us to wrap our heads around the idea that God might just want you to wave for a while—or smile at somebody. And that that honors him just as well as—if not more than—some of our grander schemes.

For the moment, you might consider the story about Waving Man to be charming or sweet. But I promise you that while you'll soon forget my attempts at enlightenment and entertainment, you'll remember his impact on the people who drive past. The effect of his life will come to you the next time you wave at a passerby.

If you have big things you think you ought to be doing but can't because it's not the right fit just now, I encourage you to chill a bit and change your perspective. For now, lower your expectations and look at what God is doing and can do with who you are where you are. This is all easier said than done, of course. But being content helps, so let's get to that.

Keys to Contentment

Talking about contentment and motherhood seems a bit off—shady almost—doesn't it? As if motherhood and children are some burdens to be endured instead of gifts to be enjoyed. As if there's no joy or reward in mothering. As if somehow we are shortchanged by the incredible gift of children.

While we *may* at times feel discontent with our role or abilities as mothers in general—or, if we're honest, at times with our kids' behavior in particular—that's not what I mean here. The contentment that needs to seep into our hearts, minds, and souls is for the hemmed-in times, when we see the hedges growing around us and feel like jumping right over them. You know, when it feels like nothing is happening, no gifts are being used, no passions are fired up, as if God has taken no consideration whatsoever of our personal temperaments when it comes to our role as mothers.

No matter how much we love everything and everyone inside our hedged yard, it's the stuff on the outside—the parts of our identities that don't seem to fit within a current season in motherhood—about which we need to seek contentment. That way, we can focus on where God wants us looking and why he wants us looking there.

For example, right now as I type, I enjoy a rare luxury: I'm alone in my house, the windows are open, and the birds outside are chirping. As my husband pulled out of the driveway with the kids just a little bit ago, I actually skipped and clapped a couple of times on my way back to my desk—I was that excited. I am nothing if not an introvert,[4] and time alone—mentally and physically—is something I crave (need actually) to recharge, to unwind, to feel like myself.

Of course, with three young kids, time alone is something I almost never get. Truth be told, it's one of the hardest parts of mothering. Ever since I was old enough to be left alone, being all by myself in an empty house has felt something like heaven to me. A time not only for refreshment but for quiet thoughts and writing or for loud music and dancing—without interruption and without, well, humiliation.

While I'm a homebody who loves feeling tucked in, all safely snuggled in the house with my husband and kids, I reach a point when being constantly surrounded and physically clung to or sat on (by my kids, not my husband) makes me near crazy. When it comes to being content in "every situation" as the apostle Paul learned to be (see Philippians 4:11), this is one situation in which finding contentment is a real struggle.

And yet God gave me three kids who more than *want* to be around me; they *need* it, of course, as all kids do. To tell you the truth, my day would stink without all the usual kid-to-mom contact of nursing, hugging, kissing, snuggling, handholding, back-rubbing, and arm-patting. But I may be able to live without the constant need for my help in every little task or game, the wanting me nearer to them than the fifteen feet between the kitchen and the living room, and the urgent questions they all seem to have at the same time. From what I can tell, none of my kids[5] has inherited my introvert gene. Quite the opposite of their mother who gets recharged from retreating, they get their charge from full-speed ahead—toward Mommy! Makes for an interesting mix.

I have a couple of choices. I can grump and groan and act all martyrish (and I do pull this off quite well) and start saving now for years of therapy for my kids and me, or I can seek contentment and try to raise kids who feel loved, valued, and like I *want* to be around them (which I do) as I try to focus on what God desires to come of this challenge to my introverted nature.

I still don't know why God—who made me this way—wouldn't give me the kind of kids who take three-hour naps until they're five (or even one-hour naps until they're two!), who can sit and color quietly for an hour, or who enjoy lengthy periods of playing alone in their rooms (and I know kids like this!). I can't be sure why it would've been so wrong to give me three night owls or three early risers instead of the mix that keeps me hopping and surrounded by small people from six in the morning until nine at night. But I'm sure glad he gave me the kids I have. I realize that if I had kids who, on a superficial level, meshed better with my temperament, it would mean I wouldn't have my Henrik, Greta, and Fredrik. No, thank you.

Aside from my God-reflecting maternal desire to see each of my children be their full selves, to live life the way God intended, I need all three—the way God made them—to shape my life the way God wants it. So I've got to trust that God knew what he was doing—and that means finding contentment in my life as it is.

While I do slip up frequently (always good to stretch those martyr muscles), I've finally taken to heart the wise words of Paul that I touched on earlier. In Philippians 4:12–13 he writes, "I know what it is to be in need, and I know what it is to have plenty. I have learned the secret of being content in any and every situation, whether well fed or hungry, whether living in plenty or in want. I can do everything through him who gives me strength."

So what's the application? What *is* the secret to contentment for moms who feel hemmed in? In verse 13, Paul seems to teach that contentment comes in strength from God. Clearly, when we're frustrated or beat down from not being able to live our identities as fully as we'd like, we can turn to God for strength. He does dole out strength by the bushelful when we're in need.

But I've got to believe there's more to Paul's secret. I ran across a new insight when I cross-referenced two totally different Bible verses. This time it was the secret-to-being-content verse considered right next to 1 Thessalonians 5:18, which says, "Give thanks in all circumstances, for this is God's will for you in Christ Jesus." Not to try to rewrite Scripture or anything, but since Paul is a master of gratitude (read his letters—the guy is *always* thanking somebody), it's not a bad guess that if Paul was content, it's at least partly because Paul was grateful.

This is where it really hits home for me as a mom—the truth is, when I eye those hedges with scorn and resentment, it means I'm not eyeing my life with gratitude. When I feel pressured by having to spend so much time with people and my introverted nature feels the walls closing in around me, the act of firing up the gratitude changes everything. This time in my life is when my kids *want* to snuggle, want to be around me, and need me close. I know the time is coming when all this will change, so I want to enjoy this stage of life to the full. I want to be thankful for it every day.

In times when I've ignored Paul's wisdom and have turned to complaining, it only makes matters worse. But I experience the total opposite effect when I ask God for strength and start praising him in the midst of what feels like chaos. Then peace prevails—always. I end up amazed at the God who loves me enough not only to give me what I need to make it through the craziness, but who tosses in a bit of fun, an obvious blessing, or a simple, doable solution to whatever I'm struggling with.

God is more than good. It's in these times of expressing gratitude and understanding contentment that he has opened my eyes, given me a clearer look not only at what might await beyond the hedges (all in good time), but at what's going on inside the boundaries. It heightens my enjoyment and appreciation for my role as a hands-on mom as well as for my wondrous and wonderful kids. It's in the times of letting go and letting God, as they say, and being content in trusting him, that he really ponies up. (And maybe one day it will be with an actual pony.)

Make the Most of the "Happy Surprises"

Two summers ago, just as I was getting into the groove of a new work-at-home position that melded my gifts, abilities, and passions more perfectly than anything I could've imagined, I discovered I was pregnant. This was a "happy surprise" (to borrow an expression from J. I. Packer) considering the conception of our first two kids required some fertility assistance. However, it was not without its bumps in the road—to match the nice bump in my midsection.

For one, while I had the work-at-home thing down to a science with my two preschoolers, I couldn't fathom how I would make it work with a new baby. I prayed about it, but all along I knew the answer. I felt God leading me to opt out, as the hip new moms say, to step back behind those hedges. I loved my part-time work arrangement, but because I knew so fully that God wanted me to step back from it, I didn't even wrestle with the decision. But I did wonder what God was up to, considering bump-in-the-road number two: our medical insurance didn't cover maternity expenses. We didn't have coverage whether I worked part-time or not, but the steady (if small) stream of money from my salaried, work-at-home gig would've come in handy with a third child on the way.

Still, my continued employment wasn't right for my kids, for my husband, or for me, so I quit two months before my little lovey Fredrik was born. Once again I settled into the contented life of the at-home mom.

Turned out, God hadn't run out of happy surprises. First came an offer from the boss I had just quit on to help shape and edit *Gifted for Leadership*, a new blog for women who lead others. It was her brainchild, but she had little time to develop the concept into reality. For me, this was an opportunity that took up very little time, offered much more flexibility, and not only used my well-practiced gifts but stretched and developed new ones. Plus, it paid. This was a much better fit than the at-home work I had let go of.

Then came my Fredrik, all smiles and personality and plumpy good looks—a Happy Surprise personified.

And then somewhere in the midst of all this, a strange man at a weekend retreat called me *mama*. It set me to thinking, and I started writing about it. And then there I was proposing a book to a variety of publishers. A happy surprise if there ever was one! Since the day I discovered Shel Silverstein's *Where the Sidewalk Ends* on a bookshelf at my godmother's house, writing has been what I wanted to do. Since I started writing later that year, at age seven, it has been how I've seen myself. Writing my own book has been a dream for almost thirty years.

Apparently, it was a dream that needed to be hemmed in for a while. Because you know what I realized? Within the hedges (and the identity crisis that ensued), God gave me the desire of my heart. He's used this time away from what I deemed as "perfect" so he could give me something better. Had I not stepped back into my hedged-in world, I would have missed out on a gift—an idea, the encouragement, the miraculous gifts of time—that God threw my way. He sent me the unexpected gift not because I'm so insightful or wise, but because he loves me, because he knows me, and because he called me to do this.

I'm not the only one who has experienced this. Big Mom Group member Valerie Weaver-Zercher describes motherhood as her "greatest Muse." I love that! Because how many of us have tapped veins of creativity we didn't know we had—inspired by the Muse of loving and watching and raising our kids? How many of us have, through this hemmed-in time, found passions and interests that we never would have discovered without the creative stimulus of motherhood?

My friend Connie Tameling took up photography after giving birth to her oldest son. It was the first time she owned a real camera, she said, as well as the first time she had "an opportunity to let the creative side that God wired into me flourish."

"I always enjoyed pencil sketching and did a bit in high school and college," she says, "but then I put it all aside during law school and throughout my career as an attorney. Once I had a good camera and a willing (well, captive at least) subject in my son, I set to work on learning the ins and outs of photography...and have spent the last six years finding my creative 'groove.'"

It's wonderful to know that God cares enough about seeing us flourish and finding a "creative groove" that he would put hedges around us so we have a chance to grow. Love that.

Last night I caught a commercial for American Express featuring Diane von Furstenberg, the wrap-dress fashion diva from the 1970s. As she walks across what looks like a snowy forest, she begins, "I didn't really know what I wanted to do..." They start flashing between scenes of leaves and fabric and tops of trees and women holding dresses as she continues in a breathy voice, "But...I knew the woman I wanted to become."

Sure, it's a *tad* dramatic and syrupy. Plus, an American Express commercial isn't normally the place I'd cop to finding inspiration, but I like what she said.

Take a look at what's frustrating you right now—the things you're not able to do right now and the dreams you want to pursue that motherhood "keeps" you from. Ask God to give you strength to endure being away from whatever these things are. Then start thanking God for everything. When you're thankful for even the most frustrating things, it brings clarity to many of the things you've been wrestling with.

As long as we know who God is—and believe that he knows what he's doing—we can rest easy in these hemmed-in times. We can grow where we are and stay ready for whatever God brings into our lives. Over time God will squeak open that little gate and lead us into another, fuller expression of our identities.

QUESTIONS FOR REFLECTION AND DISCUSSION

- What's one thing you still identify with even though you can't currently "live" it?
- How do you sense God hemming you in for his own purposes? What's your reaction to this?
- When was the last time you asked God to show you what he wants you to do during your hemmed-in periods? What did he say?
- How content would you say you are with your life at the moment? Over the past three months? How grateful are you for your life right now?
- If you decided to thank God more and complain less, what would that mean to your life—and the lives of those in your family?
- How have the hedges of motherhood sharpened your outlook for the future? How have you sensed God preparing you for something beyond those hedges?

CHAPTER 12

Secret #7:
Risk Vulnerability

We know you're not perfect.
Might as well admit it

When I graduated from college, I set out to become an advertising copywriter. I had abandoned my initial dreams of being a magazine editor after being told by enough people that it was a field that's "really hard to get into." Plus, I had spent a couple of summers writing catalog copy for Spiegel—where my dad worked—and loved it. That type of writing mimicked poetry, which was my first and still favorite form of writing. I was a poet of sorts, using concise, vivid language to get thirty-five-year-old women to buy a V-necked, formfitting, three-button Henley Tee that works at the office and dazzles on the town.

So after college, I started the rounds of "informational interviews," which essentially meant getting together for lunch with friends of my dad's who worked in the advertising business. The result was that they told me advertising copywriting was "really hard to get into."

While I appreciated the time everyone took to offer their insights, that was an incredibly discouraging summer. Until one day, when I headed into the offices of a longtime friend of my father's who worked totally outside of any writing-type industry. He was a headhunter and a well-connected guy. As I sat in his beautiful, meant-to-impress office in the Lyric Opera of Chicago on North Wacker Drive in Chicago, he asked me how the job search had been going. I don't know what overtook me—weariness of being "on" and sort of fake, I guess—but I just laid out my frustrations. I told him all about everyone's negative comments and general dream squashing.

He sat back and said, "Who cares what everyone says. What do you want to do?"

That was nice to hear, so I told him I wanted to work for a magazine; I wanted to be an editor. He didn't tell me it was too hard or paid too little or that it was a silly dream for someone who hadn't graduated from a big-deal journalism school. Instead, he started asking me what it was that I liked about magazines and what made me want to work for one. Then he asked what I thought I could bring to the table.

Because I didn't think I was being interviewed, I started answering *very* honestly about what I was good at and what I needed to work on. I spoke openly about the little I had to offer experience-wise but emphasized my weird love of—and knack for—making other people's writing better. I told him I was afraid I had blown it by going down the copywriting path instead of sticking to my original plan, since now I didn't have any editorial internships under my belt. I told him I was a good, hard worker who could be a great editor but was worried I wouldn't get the chance.

After I talked for a while, he stopped me.

"Funny that you're bringing this up," he said. "I didn't know you were interested in this. Your dad only mentioned copywriting. But I can always call the guy back..."

I thought he was having a senior moment. "What guy?" I asked.

"A guy I helped place at Maclean Hunter, the magazine publisher across the street. He called last week; he's looking for an assistant editor, very entry level..."

I have no idea what we talked about after that—my brain got kind of fuzzy, and I just remember smiling. But I did end up as the assistant editor of that magazine, *Engineering and Mining Journal,* a trade magazine proudly serving the mining industry since 1866. (And yes, I was actually *quite* excited about working there!)

My new boss (a.k.a. "the guy") later told me I got the job because I came so "highly recommended." But in my mind I got the job because I laid it all out: the good, the bad, and the ugly. It was one of my most profound lessons in the reward that can come when you risk vulnerability, when you're willing to be open and honest and real.

It's a lesson I tried to carry with me into the workplace. I found it natural to balance professionalism with being myself. I also found it professionally rewarding. I succeeded at what I set out to do essentially by being my whole, real self.

When I entered motherhood, however, this balance sort of fell apart. While our crazy postmodern world may laud authenticity—which is a good thing—and we pooh-pooh *poseurs,* when it comes to moms, we're not quite there (obviously). We moms still need practice at being genuine women, women free enough to express who we are and live it as much as we can—as much as God calls us to.

But to experience the true reward, we need to risk vulnerability on another level. We need to be women who are not held back by shame, secrets, or insecurities. We need to be willing to share our sufferings and not be afraid to dream out loud. Being this kind of woman isn't always a cakewalk, which is why we're going to spend more time here in a minute.

The reward for doing this hard work is freedom, true community, and the blessing of the life God created you for. It's not a journey that is always easy or how you imagined it would be, but one that has you growing and doing and being the mother and the woman God created you to be.

So let's find out how to get real.

Spill Your Secrets, Heal Your Soul

My friends in Twelve-Step groups have a saying I love: "You're only as sick as your secrets." I think this is not only a sound psychological saying (say *that* out loud three times!) but solid spiritual wisdom as well.

I hate to get all "beware the devil!" on you, but I believe Satan is active in the world every bit as much as I believe in the good work of God. And I know Satan loves secrets—he loves *our* secrets—because they hold us back, limit us, and prevent us from being used fully by God. Satan can take some normal failing or flaw and create such shame and regret in us that it becomes the One Big Issue that will keep us from entering into real, honest community with one another. Satan can take our secrets and use them to keep us from living the life God intended for us.

Satan is the voice that once told (or still tells) you, *God doesn't love you. You're a mess. How could God love you with all you've done?* It's easy to believe that, because every one of us has done a lot!

And yet, there's this other Voice—the True One—that says, "This is how much God loved the world: He gave his Son, his one and only Son. And this is why: so that no one need be destroyed; by believing in him, anyone can have a whole and lasting life. God didn't go to all the trouble of sending his Son merely to point an accusing finger, telling the world how bad it was. He came to help, to put the world right again" (John 3:16–17, MSG).

That's some truth! The first part of this passage is, of course, the most famous and most familiar verse in the New Testament. But this last part, about Jesus coming to save the world, not to point a finger (or "condemn it" as other Bible translations say) always gives me goose bumps. It's at once so heroic, so noble, and yet so totally loving and humbling.

And, of course, it's the total opposite of what Satan—and the world—would have us believe. Satan tries to sell us the lie that if God knew what we were *really* like, he'd never love us. This couldn't be further from the truth! He knew what we were like first—knew every wretched sin we have ever committed, are committing, or will commit—and still sent his Son to *help* us, to put us right again.

This is how we can know that the feeling we get that we need to cover up parts of our life is complete bunk. We live in fear of being rejected, ridiculed, shunned, and condemned. We believe the lie that if we come clean, take the mask off, and open up about how we really are or how our lives really are, that we won't be loved or accepted.

Of course, as with all good lies, Satan's spin has just enough truth to make it believable. The thing is, when you open up about your life or your dreams, your fears, your failings, or your sufferings, some people will criticize you, reject you, or become jealous of you. Just look at the life of Jesus! If you follow him, you're especially guaranteed this treatment from *some* people.

But the bigger truth is that *most* people will be drawn to you because of your openness and transparency. And even if some people avoid the new, honest, open you, the freedom you'll experience from pushing out from behind your secrets, the freedom from the fear and shame that once held you back, will be worth the potential hurt from a few critics.

My mom taught me that the people who can't tolerate openness and candor are jealous of the freedom that is enjoyed by those who decide to live openly and honestly. And she was right!

Your Life Set on "Open"

But what does this openness look like? Do we dredge up some horrid secrets from the past and start blathering on and on to everyone we meet? Of course not. We need to be careful to discern what constitutes "our" secrets. A world of difference lies between our opening up about our own issues and revealing those of our loved ones.

We should not go around spreading private matters about our husbands or our children just so we can "be ourselves." But I think the key here is the distinction between living a life of secrets and simply respecting privacy. It's a matter of attitude, outlook, and approach, as well as how much stock we put in maintaining our image. If you're overly concerned about protecting your image, you're not living the vulnerable life that brings freedom.

Being enslaved to our secrets means we live in fear that others will discover the truth and our image will be destroyed. Respecting privacy means we're open about the fact that we or our families have "issues," that we are far from perfect, that our lives get messy, and yet we don't need to go into details unless it's particularly warranted. We don't live in fear of being "found out," because we don't waste energy promoting the false image of perfection. By admitting we are who we are, we freely join the ranks of the flawed. And that is extremely freeing.

Nobody can tear down a wall that's not there, so we need to stop putting them up. And sometimes suffering is just the thing to make us do that.

Share your sufferings

When my parents' troubled marriage ended several years ago, among the myriad pains I felt was the simple stab of having to *tell* people. Honestly, for me nothing is harder than sharing suffering, whether it's the ache that lingers in my life or the acute pain that zaps me now and again. I'm just no good at telling people that I hurt.[1]

And it seems over the past several years there has been a lot of suffering in my life—from a huge financial reversal to emotional and psychological issues within the family (note the openness while protecting privacy?) to my own identity crisis. None of this has been easy to open up about. I have feared being the target of gossip, judgment, and rejection—as well as being seen as a constant complainer!

So for me to tell you that this sharing of your sufferings is key to becoming truly known and revealing the real you, borders on hypocrisy. I'm spared only by my recent conversion to the benefits of sharing.

A couple of things got me on this path. The first was realizing, like I mentioned before, the connections and freedom you feel when you open up about what is less-than-pleasant in your life. I remember when I first told one of my friends about my dad moving out and getting his own apartment. Her parents—in my eyes—had the perfect marriage, so her response to my telling her my news shocked me.

"Oh," she said. "My dad would *love* that!"

After we both got done laughing (though she was dead serious), we had a terrific conversation about the difficulty of not having good marriage role models and the loneliness of feeling like you need to stake out new territory on your own. This conversation—this feeling of being understood and known—held me up during a difficult time.

Each time I've shared suffering since then, no matter what the response from the other person (though it's usually supportive), I've found the freedom that comes from moving bits of your life out into the light. It's this action that keeps suffering from becoming shame—another popular tool of the devil.

Beyond that, sharing suffering deepens you in the eyes of others and provides a framework to understand, know, and even appreciate you better. An example: Last week, Miss Jane, the woman who cleans my house a couple of times a month (I figure, a few hours more freelance work is well worth the cost of paying someone to scour my kitchen!) brought a friend with her to help. I instantly loved her brightly dispositioned friend Maria—mostly because she was kind to my kids and my dog. She told us funny stories about her homeland of Romania and gave me a few etymology lessons as she explained the close linguistic relationship between the Romanian and Spanish languages. Who knew?

The other thing I never would've guessed was the measure to which this woman had suffered. A few years ago, back in Romania, her seventeen-year-old daughter died of carbon-monoxide poisoning while taking a shower. Aside from the obvious horror of losing her daughter, most everything else had gone south for Maria since then. She sought work in the United States so she could try to make the lives of her surviving kids—and their kids—better.

As shocking as the story itself was, what shocked me more was her joyful manner. I stood in amazement at this woman who has known more suffering than most of us ever will face. Yet Maria presents herself more joyfully than I do. This backdrop of profound sadness made her joy even brighter. I suspect I know her secret. It's got to be that joy that comes from serving a God who entered into suffering himself so that we might have hope and gladness even in the midst of our pain.

The greatest "triumph" that comes with sharing our suffering is the spiritual one. I was reminded of this while at a recent Taizé service at my church. The service ends with a "Prayer around the Cross," where everyone is invited to come forward and kneel in front of or touch a large wooden cross and pray—symbolically laying your burdens at the cross of Jesus and indicating by your actions that you are entrusting your burdens to him. The program explained it was a way "of expressing an invisible communion not only with the crucified Jesus, but with all who suffer."[2]

I knelt at that cross, half-crying and half-praying with my brothers and sisters in Christ as we half-publically, half-privately poured our suffering before our Lord who suffered (for us!). It changed the way I saw—and knew—those who prayed with me. Though I don't know exactly the way they suffer, knowing that they do and that they seek comfort and healing from the same great Comforter and Healer I do, deepens that sense of belonging that we all so desperately seek.

It helps us know each other better on a human and spiritual level as we lay out not only our suffering but ultimately our dreams and hopes.

Because being vulnerable and being real isn't only about opening up with the *bad* stuff, it's also about revealing the good, the fun, and the eternal promises.

Dream out Loud

My neighbor Kathryn told me one of her biggest problems with her fake I.D. is that people are shocked to discover that she actually has hopes and dreams of her *own* that have nothing (or little) to do with her family.

When she told me this, do you know what my first thought was? I thought, *You do?* Nice, huh? I mean, after all these years of hanging out on the back stoop and front porch chatting while our kids played, after all the family parties, phone calls, e-mails, Facebook status updates, I had no idea that she dreamed of getting paid to bake (which she should! I live for her Christmas cookies) or that she hoped to become a published writer (you'd think she'd have mentioned that one to her editor neighbor), or that she longed to travel internationally (though, come to think of it, who doesn't?).

I didn't know these things not because I didn't care, but because when we moms talk, we get so caught up in the here and now—understandable since most of us are just trying to make it through the day—that we rarely get to the when and if.

And yet, we usually do find time for a smidge of gossip, a funny kid story that only other moms can appreciate, or a quick vent about a family-life frustration. So why is it so hard to squeeze in a moment to talk about what we hope for in the future?

When I asked a friend about this recently, she thought it had nothing to do with time, but everything to do with fear. "Because sharing a dream," she said, "only sets us up for more failure. Yet another undone thing on that list."

Her comment struck me as totally sad but totally true. It gets back to that high-expectation thing. If we *say* we want to do something that seems so far out there or so currently unattainable, we can set ourselves up for failure. Or at the very least it might invite one of those fake-encouraging, grandmotherly "you just keep dreaming, dearie" pats on the arm. And who wants an arm-pat that shouts "Don't be so foolish, dearie!"?

But what's foolish about dreams? And what's wrong with believing in them? Walt Disney famously said, "If you can dream it, you can do it." Of course, long before Disney said this, the apostle Paul said that love "believes all things, hopes all things..." (1 Corinthians 13:7, NKJV).

Good old Walt was cryogenically frozen so he could come back one day and keep going with his dreams. I hope that works out for him (though my hopes are not high). Those of us who believe the Love of whom Paul writes have better reason to hope: without question, all of us will die long before every dream is fulfilled, every hope reached, every desire met. But the good news is that it doesn't end here.

I have no doubt that part of the wonder of heaven will be the fulfillment of the dreams that our souls harbor right now. God may have planted them in your soul to grow here on earth, to help reveal the real you, and to bring forth other good things in your life. But perhaps he never intended that you fulfill all these dreams in this life.

I may never own a horse this side of heaven. I may never get to spend my summers in Ephraim, Wisconsin, passing the days reading out on a sturdy pier and writing in a beautiful room that overlooks Green Bay. I may never see my parents' marriage restored or other relationships healed. I may never write the things I dream of writing, go the places I long to go, or meet the people I'd love to meet. But still, these dreams are worth sharing—as points of connection, perhaps ways of seeing them met—whether for this life or the next.

Especially since our dreams and hopes aren't always about things we long to do or accomplish, but about the way we long to be or to feel, a pain we wish would go away, a love we wish would come, or a peace we wish would prevail—in our personal life or on earth. A key part of being known as the real you is sharing those dreams and hopes, even when doing so feels a bit "out there" or just plain scary.

And that's the thing about revealing the real you in general: it *is* scary and takes courage—no doubt about that. It's easier to leave things status quo. It's easier to remain hidden behind the world of expectations and stereotypes. It's easier not to figure out who you really are and what word should come at the end of "I'm a mom and a __ ." But boy, oh boy, do you miss out—on community, on being known and loved for who you are, and on the blessings that come with the life God intended for you as a mom and beyond.

When all is said and done, the best thing you can do to lose the fake I.D. is to toss it out yourself. My friend Tracey says we need to learn to just "bring it." I love that.

My friend Anne says it another way: "I am just what I am—face value."

These attitudes, in fact, reflect all seven secrets to living as God made you. Because bringing it and being who you are at face value means being open, being vulnerable, and taking a risk to enjoy a reward.

Which brings us to just one more thing: once you're on the road to revealing the real you and reveling in the reward, you've got some "pay it forward" work to do. In Luke 12:48, Jesus says, "From everyone who has been given much, much will be demanded; and from the one who has been entrusted with much, much more will be asked."

Tell you what, sisters: this means that this new, real I.D. you've been given comes with responsibility and expectations—to reach out and help other moms who are trapped as you once were. All moms need to know that God created us special with a purpose that extends beyond motherhood—and that it's okay to want to be known and loved for who God made us to be.

So before we bid *adieu*, let's see how we can become even more of ourselves by becoming blessings to others.

QUESTIONS FOR REFLECTION AND DISCUSSION

- Think about some of your secrets. In what ways do they drag you down and steal your sense of well-being?
- How scary is it for you to think about opening up about your secrets? How can you get over the uneasiness?
- What sorts of secrets or sufferings are hardest for you to share? Why?
- Who are the people in your life who know your dreams and ambitions? Why do they—and not certain other people—know about these dreams?
- Think about times you have taken the risk to open up with others. What rewards did you enjoy as a result?

PART 3

Get Out
There and
Be a Blessing

CHAPTER 13

How to Help Other Moms Get Real

It's one of the best things you can do for your friends

My pastor, Bert DeJong, is the fourth of eight children born to a family of Dutch immigrants. So when he tells a story about his growing-up years, you know you're going to get some crazy, big-family "comedy" mixed with old-school, no-frills, hard-life immigrant wisdom.

A few Sundays back we heard one of these stories—this time about birthday traditions. Specifically about the way things went down on his unfortunate birthday—April 1. As you might imagine, instead of a nice chorus of "Happy Birthday" sung by loving siblings as he came down to breakfast on his big day, he was greeted with a practical joke, laughter at his expense, and his siblings yelling "April Fools!"

Apparently, however, he grew up unscarred by this. Partly because he knew his brothers and sisters loved him; partly because he knew he'd be doing the same thing if it were a sibling's birthday. But mostly because his mom knew how to make his birthday something special.

Part of the celebration for each child in his family was to hear their mother recount the day of their birth (very impressive for a woman with eight kids, don't you think?). My pastor's mom would tell him these three things: One, it was springtime. Two, it was the end of World War II. And three, it was Easter Sunday.

Okay. When Pastor Bert told us these three things, I had the same reaction you're probably having now: *Huh? That's it? Even with eight kids, you'd* think *she could come up with something better than that!*

But then he clarified. We needed to understand that he was born in the Netherlands in 1945. The springtime into which he was born followed the Hunger Winter when some twenty thousand Dutch people died of starvation during the Nazi occupation. This also makes the end of World War II all the more important: Canadian forces had liberated Bert's city just before he was born. And the Easter Sunday thing? Just something rare and special.

His mother mentioned these three things so her son would know why his particular birth day was so special—for her and for him. His birth marked not only the usual joy of a new baby, but also a time of liberation and rebirth both for a war-ravaged country and a terrified young mother. Of course, with Easter, his birth also marked the promise of liberation and rebirth for everyone else.

Our pastor said his mother's words blessed him. And he meant literally. She intended her words as a blessing to her son—something Bert defined as "being affirmed for who you are."

I thought this was spectacular—a terrific illustration of one of a mother's most important roles: blessing her children, telling them that not only is it okay to be who they are, but that they are loved especially *because* of who they are.

And then Pastor Bert talked about what it means to bless others— and be blessed. Apparently, the word *blessing* in Greek *(eulogia)* means "praise, fine speaking." The power to bless lies in words that "communicate approval and empower the person for what God put them on earth to do," he said.

My heart raced a bit as I worked through the ways I empowered my kids through blessings—and the ways I needed to do better. And then my pastor said the words that *nearly* made me jump up and shout "Hallelujah!" "When you bless someone," he said, "you give them a picture of themselves that is honest, affirming, and empowering. That's a blessing!"[1]

So while I wasn't shouting out loud, inside I was shouting *hallelujah!* At this point I was thinking beyond[2] all the ways I could give my kids honest, affirming, and empowering pictures of themselves. I was thinking, *We moms gotta do this for each other! We gotta bless each other—give each other this honest, affirming, and empowering picture of who God made us to be. That's the* real *secret.*

Blessing each other *is* the real secret. When we use words to communicate to women that they are more than moms, that we see all that God made them to be, all that they can be, we bless them.

So here's the thing, my friends: after all these chapters of thinking about ourselves (in a good way!), of searching our hearts, minds, and souls, we've got to get this show on the road. It's time to reach out.

The good news about this whole blessing business, this reaching out to affirm and empower women to do what God put them on earth to do, is that it's simple and straightforward. We bless other moms and help them live out their true identities by applying the Golden Rule. Ask them about the same things you wish other women would ask of you. Affirm them in ways you'd like to be affirmed. Empower them as you'd like to be empowered.

This doesn't require any huge new ministry launches. Blessing other women—helping them shine as the women they were made to be—simply requires your words. We're talking about a conversation! Whenever you speak to another mom in the course of your week (and don't feel bad if you don't—we've all been there!), you can do this. You can help that mom. In fact, I think you're called to help her, as an act of love.

You know, when one of the "teachers of the law" asked Jesus to identify the greatest commandment—in one of many attempts to snare him—he said, "The first in importance is, 'Listen, Israel: The Lord your God is one; so love the Lord God with all your passion and prayer and intelligence and energy.' And here is the second: 'Love others as well as you love yourself.' There is no other commandment that ranks with these" (Mark 12:29–31, MSG).

What we've been talking about up to this point has everything to do with that first commandment—us loving God with everything he gave us, in a way only we can. But since Jesus doesn't stop there, neither should we. We're told to love others as we love ourselves—back to the Golden Rule.

Paul expands on this a bit in Galatians 5:13–15: "It is absolutely clear that God has called you to a free life. Just make sure that you don't use this freedom as an excuse to do whatever you want to do and destroy your freedom. Rather, use your freedom to serve one another in love; that's how freedom grows. For everything we know about God's Word is summed up in a single sentence: Love others as you love yourself. That's an act of true freedom. *If you bite and ravage each other, watch out*—in no time at all you will be annihilating each other, and where will your precious freedom be then?" (MSG, emphasis added)

Again, this passage highlights the "free life" we're called to live and the importance of serving one another in that free life. But since he doesn't end there—and instead goes into a bit of a "dark place"—I don't think we should end there either.

Before we get to the ways we moms can and ought to bless one another, I want to back up a bit—close to where we were when we were pointing out, in chapter 5, the church's blind spots—and see what happens when we fail to bless one another.

When Moms Attack

Okay, so maybe moms are not out there biting and ravaging each other at playgroups and school functions *per se*, but we've got to be upfront about this. We moms are not always the most supportive of one another. How many times have you looked at another mom's parenting style, career choice, or personal lifestyle and decided to take her to task in your mind? We do it all the time. Moms can be classic bullies—putting other moms down to lift ourselves up, right?

In fact, my friend Carla told me she thinks we moms are a huge part of the whole stereotyping, fake I.D. problem to begin with. "We quickly pick out those moms we think are like us and those we think are not [like us] based on the most trivial things—what kind of clothes or diapers our kids wear, if we nurse or bottle feed, how we discipline, how stressed out we seem, how put together we are. I am totally guilty of this myself. Of course, I am more likely to be friends with moms who are on the same page as me on some of these things, but I don't think it's good for us to make these determinations so quickly or create little categories in our heads about who has it right and who doesn't."[3]

Members of my Big Mom Group have said they struggle the most with personal identity problems when they're with other moms, second only to being in church. Maybe because we're all struggling, it makes it tough to accept one another when we get together.

But something struck me as I did research for this book, particularly as I poured through answers and comments given to me by my Big Mom Group, as well as other women I chatted with. I'm in contact with women who could not be more different from one another when it comes to the things Carla talked about—on issues of nursing, discipline, stress, diapers, work, among others—yet who struggle in exactly the same areas, with the same feelings of anonymity, isolation, and not being valued for their gifts.

I remember several times thinking, *These women might never be friends because of the "trivial things."* Yet their answers to my questions of identity and motherhood reflected a deep-down value and longing for the same acceptance. Two moms might have a falling-out over cloth diapers vs. disposables or homeschooling vs. public schools, but in their heart of hearts both moms want exactly the same thing.

My favorite—and the most glaring—example of this was two members of the Big Mom Group whom I knew to be at opposite ends of the political spectrum. I can guarantee they have never and probably will never vote for the same candidate or agree on the same public-policy issues. And yet, as I looked over their answers to my survey, I realized how alike they are. They share a deep commitment to their role as hands-on, at-home moms and an even deeper love for their kids. And they both gave almost identical responses when talking about how their sacrifices as committed, loving moms affect them and their sense of who they are.

The quest for belonging and acceptance transcends so much else—the fringe issues just aren't that important. If we can extend this grace of getting to know other women, of drawing them out, instead of disparaging them because they have no problem buying war toys for their boys, we moms can do such a huge amount of good. For general society, for this country, and for the whole kingdom of God here on earth. We can change a generation of moms and tilt the culture in favor of moms by being a blessing when we talk with other moms.

Give an Honest Picture

According to my pastor, the first step in blessing people is to give them an honest picture of themselves. This does not mean it's open season on criticism. I know, for example, that I don't actually need one more person to tell me I "look tired." I've got that. Thanks!

Instead, it's more like the statement that is commonly attributed to Hilary Price, author of *The Life That Changed My Day:* "One of the biggest problems with [Christian] women is that they are not honest with themselves or those around them."[4] Now that we are moms with real I.D.'s, we can change this. We now know how to be honest with ourselves—so it's time to be honest with those around us. We tackled this in the last chapter when we talked about risking vulnerability. One of the other things that our own vulnerability does, however, is create an environment for others to be real and honest.

So while giving another mom an honest picture of herself doesn't mean we need to tell her that her stretched-out skin looks gross (at least, I don't want to hear this); it means creating a culture of honesty in which she can express herself openly and then see herself more clearly. It's a safe environment that allows her to unload her weaknesses and share her strengths—and find encouragement in both.

One year at our local MOPS meetings, the group leader would start each discussion time with something called "Bag It or Brag It." Essentially, it was a time to either unload or exult. This was my favorite thing, quite honestly. It was so terrific to have a place where you could safely fess up to messing up royally as well as collect some pats on the back for being a great mom.

Every conversation we women have should include this, I think. But to make it work, to create a safe enough environment for this part of blessing to occur, a few things need to be in place.

One: We need to cut out gossiping—entirely—from our conversations. If you think you don't gossip, that's fine, but take it from this recovering gossip (who certainly falls off the wagon now and again!) that it's not always easy to spot in oneself. So stop a minute and really look at the things you chat about. The classic standard for measuring gossip is "if you're part of neither the solution nor the problem, then it's gossip." Proverbs 16:28 says gossip separates friends, so that's another good gauge. You can also apply the Golden Rule—would you like others talking about you the way you're talking about them?

All this to say, when you gossip, you become unsafe. No one will risk vulnerability around you, so you will be prevented from blessing them by offering honesty.

Two: We need to empathize with other moms even when we don't relate to their situations, understand their challenges, or even fully agree with their complaints. As long as you don't feel their choices are morally wrong, you can "walk" alongside them and offer public support. This means defending their privacy and fending off gossip.

Three: We need to offer truth without harshness. You know, the whole truth-in-love thing. So that when someone comes to us with what's on her heart, we can offer her a real picture of herself, but one that's cushioned in kindness.

And four: Keep it real yourself, which means living your life as a blessing. I came *this close* to ending this list at three pointers because we've talked about this stuff already. But then I read two bits of wisdom (read them just below) and was reminded of the importance of an honest blessing.

The first was this nugget, which I read at *Memoir of a Misfit* author Marcia Ford's Web site: "Most of the time I have felt out of place in church, but I want to emphasize that I'm not blaming 'the church' for that. The church is us, and we make each other feel out of place. I'm sure I've done unto others what I wish they had not done unto me. Again, I think it's partly because we feel as if everyone else has it together, that there's this code that everyone else knows, and in our desperation to discover that code for ourselves, we end up hurting ourselves and others by creating this mythical 'ideal Christian.' The gospel gets reduced to a call to conformity as a result, and God has to hate that."[5]

And then I reread a comment that Kathy, a member of my Big Mom Group, made: "I hate when [my family's] all fighting, and then we head off to church, acting like we are all happy and put together when we arrive." This almost made me laugh out loud because if indeed there were some secret code, as Marcia alludes to, to being the "ideal Christian," Kathy would know it! She comes from good solid Christian stock—one of those generations-of-faith families most of us can only dream of.

I want us to be real, but I'm not suggesting that you continue screaming at your kids as you walk from the church parking lot into the foyer, just to be authentic. But I did enjoy hearing Kathy talk about this. While Sunday mornings have long been documented as the most racially and ethnically segregated time of the week in America, they also have to be the fakest. I don't know about you, but Sunday mornings get *bad* at my house. Especially the last fifteen minutes before we need to leave. It's all stress and yelling and rushing and annoyance (and most of this comes directly from me!).

I think Kathy and Marcia are tapping into the same point, though. Church isn't always a safe place for honesty, for being real. So we can bless other moms by bringing it—maybe even by affirming all it takes (i.e., the screaming and the gnashing of teeth) to get a family to church in the first place.

Affirm Another Mom

So not to stereotype here, but affirmation is something moms have down pretty pat, right? I mean, it's as crucial to the good-mom role as love and kisses. (Though, on a side note, I do know one mom who never gives her beautiful, smart children better than a "you're fine" grade to keep them from becoming "too confident." I'm sure she has her reasons, but yikes!) I mean, we moms start affirming our kids from the moment they're born and go on to smiling and praising good burps and big toots, through celebrating milestones—big and small—all the way up to rewarding good report cards and good choices on sex and illegal substances. To this day, when I need affirmation, I go to my mom!

So when it comes to my pastor's second suggestion for how to bless one another, we're pretty good to go. Because it's not only our kids we affirm easily, it's other moms. We're quick to compliment a new haircut, a cute outfit, weight lost, a good recipe, a beautiful garden. We notice well-behaved kids and all the hard work moms are doing. I think because we know what a thankless job motherhood is and how invisible most of us are, we do go out of our way to call attention to and praise what moms are doing for their families.

The challenge is to take this deeper and further: to affirm one another beyond the obvious, beyond what meets the eye, and beyond our roles as moms. To do it well, we really need to take it up a notch, to be on the lookout to affirm not only the obvious but also things that aren't immediately apparent—but without prying. It means more than complimenting what's clear to the naked eye, but drawing other moms out, asking questions that help you see what others may not—and affirm that.

I'm borrowing one of the best techniques for this from marriage advice I used to read all the time when I edited *Marriage Partnership* magazine. When I worked there, I didn't have kids, so the advice to "*never* talk about your kids when you're out on a date with your husband" struck me as silly, if not borderline cruel. Of course, now that I've got kids, I get it. Totally. Because when you're talking about the kids, you're not talking about the "us" that is you and your husband.

So one of the best ways, I think, to get to affirming other moms is to make your own personal "rule" to not talk about kids when you're out with a friend. You don't need to be obnoxious about enforcing this, but if you swirl around in your head the idea that when you do talk kids, it can be harder to affirm your friend, it becomes easier.

When kids don't dominate a conversation, you have time to ask your friend all the questions you've asked yourself throughout this book—and more. You can get to know another person. You can verbally affirm her gifts and who she is outside of her mom role.

Before we head on to empowering one another, one last thing about affirmation: it's through being affirmed that we know what we're good at. I mean, we may *feel* we have a certain gift or talent or calling, but it's usually someone else's affirmation of that gift that makes it real. And if we want to empower or be empowered, we need to be dealing with what is real.

Go Out and Empower Somebody

This is the part that charges me up the most. I love the idea of moms empowering one another. But I also know this is the part that scares people the most. We may have come a long way, baby, but let's face it, when women start talking "empowerment," plenty of people get nervous. For many, the idea of "empowering women" still brings to mind kicking men to the curb, or radicalized women burning their bras, or a general approach to life that is inherently anti-family and anti-Christian.

This drives me nuts. If anybody should know about—and experience—empowerment, it's Christians. Empowering one another—to live as God called us to—is part of our Christian calling. As a matter of fact, in 2 Timothy 1:7 we read: "God did not give us a spirit of timidity, but a spirit of power, of love and of self-discipline." I like the way *The Message* renders this verse: "God doesn't want us to be shy with his gifts, but bold and loving and sensible."

And 1 Thessalonians 5:8–11 says, "Let us be self-controlled, putting on faith and love as a breastplate, and the hope of salvation as a helmet. For God did not appoint us to suffer wrath but to receive salvation through our Lord Jesus Christ. He died for us so that, whether we are awake or asleep, we may live together with him. Therefore encourage one another and build each other up, just as in fact you are doing."

We're talking about a spirit of power. Think about it: breastplates, helmets, encouraging one another, and building each other up—these are not timid, retiring, apologetic things. That's empowerment! But we don't always see others bending over backward to help moms with this sort of thing. Which means, just as we've had to do with so many other things, we need to take the initiative to get it done! As we live as the gifted, individual women God made us to be, it's up to us to bless other women through empowering them.

So what does this look like? It means creating safe environments and being generous with affirmation. But ultimately we're talking about being women who give other moms the confidence, help, and guidance to live as the women God intended them to be. Since to *empower* means simply to enable or "to promote the...influence of,"[6] this takes many shapes: from baby-sitting so your friend can indulge a passion to publically praising someone who might be shy about revealing her gifts. It's any way you can enable someone to live as God called her to.

Often, it is simply through our words. Earlier I mentioned that my friend Amy, a publishing industry insider, spoke the words every aspiring author longs to hear: "You should write a book about that." She not only affirmed me, but she empowered me. Her continued encouragement and guidance through the initial stages allowed this book to be. She was an empowerer—and, I believe, an instrument of God, since without her words, encouragement, and help I wouldn't have had the confidence to go forward.

For my friend Carla, empowering means helping others carry their loads, knowing that "when we allow others to shine as brightly as we'd like to think we shine, everyone wins."[7]

You know, the best part of blessing other moms is that we all win. Others win, of course, by being blessed, but we also get blessed by getting to share in another person's God-ordained story. Pretty exciting stuff when you think that God has ordained each of us to share his grace and love and to transform this world for him! We're called to do it certainly through our children and through our roles as moms, but in all the other ways you've discovered as well. When we are able to help other women, through honesty and affirmation, to discover and reveal who God made them to be—and then empower them to be it—we interlink our stories, our purposes, without giving up our individuality. With the beautiful individual pieces we bring, we become part of a grander, spectacular mosaic or maybe a puzzle of purpose that God's got going on.

In her book *Nice Girls Don't Change the World*, Lynne Hybels shares the famous Margaret Mead quote: "Never doubt that a small group of thoughtful, committed citizens can change the world."[8] Then below it, she writes, "My version of that quote is: Never doubt that a community of thoughtful, committed women, filled with the power and love of God, using gifts they have identified and developed, and pursuing passions planted in them by God—never doubt that these women can change the world."[9]

Indeed.

And that's really what this identity stuff is all about—the ways that God made us, as individuals, to change the world! It sounds lofty and certainly overwhelming (especially when we're knee-deep in mommy duty) but it's the truth. It's why we were put here in the first place. Remember, God made you the way he did to meet needs (feed hungry stomachs, hang with lonely people, seek justice) and reach people (those who are hurting and suffering and desperate for saving grace) all in his name, in your own way. Same as he did for all the other women we need to be blessing through our honest pictures and our words of affirmation and empowerment.

Whew. That's a tall order. But a great one—and the key to a blessed life yourself.

So, my fellow moms, here's a quick blessing for you: May you live and be loved, valued, and known as the women God made you to be. May you never be ashamed of or try to stifle the gifts God gave you and the passions he put in your heart. May it always be that all us mamas are wearing our real I.D.'s.

Now go kiss your kids!

QUESTIONS FOR REFLECTION AND DISCUSSION

○ In what way do you bless your kids with your words?

○ Have you ever felt demeaned or judged by other moms? How so? What was the outcome?

○ What sorts of "petty" differences might you need to overcome so you can bless other moms?

○ What sort of praise or affirmation do you regularly give other moms?

○ Who is one mom you think needs your blessing or affirmation right now? How might you bless her?

The Big Mom Group Survey

This is an abridged version of the questionnaire I gave to the women in my Big Mom Group. They were not required to answer every question, though some did. In many ways, their answers—both the simple and profound—shaped this book (and fueled ideas for many other books!). The wisdom of these women blew me away and certainly helped me with a lot of "answers" I was looking for.

I would encourage you to answer the questions yourself. It's an interesting exercise that will open your eyes to some truths about who you are and some of the challenges you face. If you are using this book as a starting point for discussions with other moms, make use of this survey to spur further discussion.

And if you're so inclined, feel free to e-mail me your answers at caryn@carynrivadeneira.com. I'd love to hear from you! A slightly modified version of this survey can also be found at my Web site: www.caryn rivadeneira.com.

General Information

Are you married or a single mom?

How many kids do you have?

What are their ages?

How about gender?

Do you work (for a paycheck)? Yes/No
    If yes:
    Do you work part-time or full-time?

    From home, outside the home, or a little of both?

    For whom do you work?

    What do you do?

About Being a Mom

What is your favorite thing (or things) about being a mom?

What is your favorite thing about being known as a mom?

What is your least favorite thing about being known as a mom?

In what ways do people know you better by thinking of you as a
mom?

In what ways do people know you less well by thinking of you as a
mom?

About Mom Stereotypes

Which of the following "mom labels" do you relate to (check all that
apply)?
___at-home mom
___working mom (outside the home)
___work-at-home mom
___mompreneur
___alpha mom
___soccer mom
___hybrid mom
___beta mom
___stepmom
___single mom
___other _____

What are some of the ways labels like these help others get to know
the real you?

What are some ways that labels such as these hinder others from getting to know the real you?

When you think of the stereotypical mom, what words come to mind?

Which of these words (or which parts of the image) fit who you are?

Which words (or which parts of the image) don't fit who you are?

About Your Sense of Self

When do you feel most alive and energized as a woman? (Or describe a time or situation when you felt most like the real you.)

What do you do to recharge or get refreshed?

What would you describe as your gifts?

In what areas do your gifts mesh well with mothering?

In what areas do they not mesh all that well?

I have struggled with a common challenge of motherhood, namely the "loss of self." Can you relate to that? If yes, how so?

Can you describe a time when you felt that motherhood stripped you of yourself or your personal identity?

Is there a circumstance, setting, or situation in which you regularly struggle with your identity or have trouble fitting in as the real you? Yes/No

Is there a group of people in whose presence you struggle with your identity or have trouble fitting in as the real you? Yes/No

When I have felt stripped of my self and my identity, it has left me feeling lonely and isolated (two common "side effects" of motherhood!). How have those situations made you feel?

In what ways has motherhood helped shape your sense of self?

What are some important things people need to know about you in
order to know the "real you"?

Recommended Resources

These are books I love. Some have to do with mothering, some with women in general, and some are much more random—but all touch on our identities in one way or another.

Anderson, Joan. *A Weekend to Change Your Life: Find Your Authentic Self After a Lifetime of Being All Things to All People*. New York: Broadway, 2006.

Barnhill, Carla. *The Myth of the Perfect Mother: Rethinking the Spirituality of Women*. Grand Rapids: Baker, 2004.

Barnhill, Julie Ann. *Motherhood: The Guilt That Keeps on Giving*. Eugene, OR.: Harvest House, 2006.

Eller, T. Suzanne. *The Mom I Want to Be: Rising Above Your Past to Give Your Kids a Great Future*. Eugene, OR.: Harvest House, 2006.

Fincher, Jonalyn Grace. *Ruby Slippers: How the Soul of a Woman Brings Her Home*. Grand Rapids: Zondervan, 2007.

Fields, Leslie Leyland. *"Parenting Is Your Highest Calling" and 8 Other Myths That Trap Us in Worry and Guilt*. Colorado Springs, CO: WaterBrook, 2008.

James, Carolyn Custis. *The Gospel of Ruth: Loving God Enough to Break the Rules*. Grand Rapids: Zondervan, 2008.

Lamott, Anne. *Operating Instructions: A Journal of My Son's First Year*. New York: Pantheon, 1993.

Morgan, Elisa and Carol Kuykendall. *What Every Mom Needs*. Grand Rapids: Zondervan, 2006.

Savage, Jill. *Real Moms…Real Jesus: Meet the Friend Who Understands.*
     Chicago: Moody, 2009.

Sayers, Dorothy L. *Are Women Human? Penetrating, Sensible, and Witty
     Essays on the Role of Women in Society.* Grand Rapids: Eerdmans,
     2005.

Woolf, Virginia. *A Room of One's Own.* New York: Harcourt Brace
     Jovanovich, 1929.

Notes

Introduction

1. Rev. Carlene Appel, comment on Amy Simpson, "Why I Don't Do Women's Ministry," Gifted for Leadership blog, comment posted August 28, 2007, http://blog.christianitytoday.com/gifted forleadership/2007/08/why_i_dont_do_womens_ministry.html, used by permission.
2. See Genesis 2:18–25.
3. According to Parenthood.com, the most common complaints of stay-at-home moms "have to do with loneliness and sense of self," "Thinking About Being a Stay-at-Home Mom?" www.parenthood.com/articles.html?article_id=2713.
4. April, comment on Caryn Rivadeneira, "Identity Crisis," Gifted for Leadership blog, comment posted May 1, 2007, http://blog.christianitytoday.com/giftedforleader ship/2007/04/identity_crisis.html#comments, used by permission.

Chapter 1

1. Shayne Moore, "Leading with One Voice," March 12, 2007, http://blog.christianitytoday.com/giftedforleadership/2007/03/leading_with_one_voice.html, used by permission.
2. Moore, "Leading with One Voice."
3. Carla Barnhill, "The Wonder of the First Year," *Christian Parenting Today,* November/December 1998, www.christianitytoday.com/cpt/8g6/8g6030.html.
4. Caryn Rivadeneira, "Getting to Know God," December 29, 2007, http://carynrivadeneira.com/?p=72.

5. Angela C., comment on Caryn Rivadeneira, "Getting to Know God," comment posted December 31, 2007, http://caryn rivadeneira.com/?p=72, used by permission.

Chapter 2

1. Margaret Mitchell, *Gone with the Wind* (New York: Scribner, 2007), 577.
2. Dorothy L. Sayers, "The Human-Not-Quite-Human," in *Are Women Human?* (Grand Rapids, MI: Eerdmans, 1971), 61.
3. Sayers, "The Human-Not-Quite-Human," 62.
4. Carla Barnhill, *The Myth of the Perfect Mother* (Grand Rapids. MI: Baker, 2004), 17–18.
5. Jonalyn Grace Fincher, *Ruby Slippers: How the Soul of a Woman Brings Her Home* (Grand Rapids, MI: Zondervan, 2007), 16–17.
6. Oprah has said the issue of "loss of self" is "nearly epidemic" among moms. *The Oprah Winfrey Show,* "The Big Weigh In: Best Life Weight Loss Challenge Update," First broadcast May 22, 2007.
7. Barnhill, *The Myth of the Perfect Mother,* 77.

Chapter 3

1. Keith Green and Melody Green, "There Is a Redeemer," copyright © 1982, EMI Christian Music Group.

Chapter 4

1. See Genesis 1:27.
2. Sharon A. Hersh, "Only the Lonely," MomSense, November/December 2006, www.christianitytoday.com/momsense/2006/006/6.26.html.
3. Traditional, "Zacchaeus Was a Wee Little Man," public domain.
4. The story is found in Luke 19:1–10.
5. Randy Alcorn, *Heaven* (Carol Stream, IL: Tyndale, 2004), 278.

6. Alcorn, *Heaven,* 278.

7. Rick Warren, *The Purpose Driven Life* (Grand Rapids, MI: Zondervan, 2002), 17.

8. C. S. Lewis, *Mere Christianity* (New York: Collier, 1952), 174.

9. See Matthew 25:14–30.

10. Caryn Rivadeneira, "Rethinking Women's Ministry," Christian BibleStudies.com, www.christianbiblestudies.com.

11. This doesn't mean I don't think Jesus appreciated and welcomed Martha's form of worship in service. He rebuked her only after she complained about it!

12. For more on this idea, see Rivadeneira, "Rethinking Women's Ministry."

13. Note to Annual Fund Drive telemarketers: Sorry I've been stingy with the dough these last few years. Please consider this nice shout-out and free publicity my annual gift. Thank you.

14. Tracey Bianchi, "Should I Keep Going? Going the Extra Mile in Leadership," MOPS, www.mops.org/page.php?pageid=1646, emphasis added.

15. Sybil MacBeth, quoted in Robin Gallaher Branch, "Doodling with Devotion," *Christianity Today,* January 2008, www.ct library.com/ct/2008/january/30.61.html.

Chapter 5

1. April, comment on Caryn Rivadeneira, "Identity Crisis," Gifted for Leadership blog. Comment posted May 1, 2007, http://blog .christianitytoday.com/giftedforleadership/2007/04/identity _crisis.html#comments, used by permission.

Chapter 6

1. Stephen Colbert, *I Am America (And So Can You!)* (New York: Grand Central, 2007), 9.

2. One of my favorite answers. For me, this sums up the fake I.D. mama's got perfectly!

3. Another favorite. Though this one fits me just fine!

4. In all fairness, he would probably say the same thing since my story—a scary one about a woman, named Dimitry of all things, who rode a motorcycle with a ghost—was wretched. But still…

5. Julie Ann Barnhill, *Motherhood: The Guilt that Keeps on Giving* (Eugene, OR: Harvest House, 2006), 37–38.

6. Barnhill, *Motherhood,* 52.

7. There are no magic words to use in a prayer confessing your sin and placing your faith in Christ. Just tell God what's on your heart, and let him know you want to receive his love, grace, mercy, and forgiveness. Here are some words to help get you started. God will help you finish. "Dear God [or Jesus, Lord, Heavenly Father]: I've messed up a lot of things in my life. I feel miles away from you, but long to get close. So yes, I believe—that you died for me, that your death was the only true sacrifice for my sins, and that you rose again—and I accept your grace and forgiveness. Please be my God and help me follow you…," and just keep praying. And repenting. And grab a Bible. The gospel according to St. Mark is a good place to start.

Chapter 7

1. Barb, comment on Caryn Rivadeneira, "Your Identity in Christ," comment posted January 30, 2008, www.carynrivadeneira .com/?p=78, used by permission.

2. Siska, comment on www.GiftedForLeadership.com, April 29, 2007, www.giftedforleadership.com, used by permission.

3. Al Hsu, comment on Caryn Rivadeneira, "Your Identity in Christ," comment posted January 24, 2008, www.carynrivadeneira.com, used by permission.

4. Barb Brouwer, comment on Caryn Rivadeneira, "Your Identity in Christ," comment posted January 30, 2008, www.caryn rivadeneira.com, used by permission.

5. C. S. Lewis, *Mere Christianity* (New York: Collier, 1943), 173.

Chapter 8

1. Joan Anderson's story is worth reading—for the entertainment value alone, but also for her keen insights. The good read is reason enough, but seeing what happens if we *don't* deal with our identity issues at this stage in the game is even better!

2. Arlene F. Harder, "The Development Stages of Eric Erikson," LearningPlaceOnline.com, www.learningplaceonline.com/stages/ organize/Erikson.htm.

3. E. H. Erikson, "Reflections on the dissent of contemporary youth," *International Journal of Psychoanalysis* 51 (1970), 11–22. Cited in Kendra Van Wagner, "Identity Crisis: Theory and Research," About.com: Psychology, http://psychology.about.com/ od/theoriesofpersonality/a/identitycrisis.htm.

4. Van Wagner, "Identity Crisis."

5. Van Wagner, "Identity Crisis."

Chapter 9

1. I'm not saying euphemistically that I write while "sitting on the toilet." I mean that I am balanced on the edge of the toilet—with the lid down, of course.

2. I think you might like it too. Do yourself a favor and check out www.hybridmom.com!

3. Of course, we are all fully moms and fully *many* other things, but tacking on too many words to "a mom and a __" can get tedious.

4. "Christ-Like Answers to Annoying Questions," June 3, 2008, http://blog.christianitytoday.com/giftedforleadership/2008/06/christlike_answers_to_annoying.html.

5. Nikki A. Toyama and Tracey Gee, eds., *More Than Serving Tea: Asian American Women on Expectations, Relationships, Leadership and Faith* (Downers Grove, IL: InterVarsity, 2006), 34.

6. Toyama and Gee, *More Than Serving Tea,* 34.

7. Toyama and Gee, *More Than Serving Tea,* 34.

Chapter 10

1. That is, it's Swedish, but my 1970s-era parents apparently didn't think a Swedish pronunciation was different enough. The usual Karin had to be *spelled* differently—as Caryn—to really do the trick!

2. This passage, in slightly different form, first appeared in Caryn Rivadeneira, "It's All in My Name," *Marriage Partnership,* Summer 2000, 4, used by permission.

3. Julie Clawson, "Why I Gave My Daughter a Strong Name," Faith in a Dress blog, May 30, 2007, http://faithinadress.blogspot.com/2007/05/why-i-gave-my-daughter-strong-name.html.

4. Donald Miller, quoted in Patton Dodd, "A Better Storyteller," *Christianity Today,* June 1, 2007, www.ctlibrary.com/ct/2007/june/10.28.html.

Chapter 11

1. Rosalie G., comment on Caryn Rivadeneira, "Identity Crisis," Gifted for Leadership blog, comment posted April 29, 2007, http://blog.christianitytoday.com/giftedforleadership/2007/04/identity_crisis.html#comments, (accessed May 5, 2007), used by permission.

2. Blair Anderson, "Too Busy to Wave?" Gifted for Leadership blog,

February 15, 2008, http://blog.christianitytoday.com/giftedfor
leadership/2008/02/too_busy_to_wave.html, used by permission.

3. JoHannah, comment on "Too Busy to Wave?" Gifted for Leadership blog, comment posted February 18, 2008, http://blog
.christianitytoday.com/giftedforleadership/2008/02/too_busy
_to_wave.html, used by permission.

4. I would caution any of my fellow introverts against using this for
your "mom and a __" introduction. The conversation goes really
flat after you drop this little morsel about yourself!

5. Here I speak of the older two. My baby, Fredrik, could be hugely
introverted and just not have much of a choice. I need to keep
him within eyeshot too!

Chapter 12

1. I try to be careful when using this word, since I have not known
true suffering the way many in the world have. Were I to know
what it was to see my children die because I could not feed them, I
would not consider my troubles suffering. I realize it is all relative.

2. Description taken from *Taizé: Songs for Prayer,* (France: Ateliers et
Presses de Taizé, 1998), Assembly Edition by GIA Publications.

Chapter 13

1. These ideas are paraphrased and abridged from a sermon given by
Rev. Bert DeJong, senior pastor of Elmhurst Christian Reformed
Church in Elmhurst, Illinois, used by permission.

2. I have since thought about this much more. Didn't want you to
think I was done blessing the kids.

3. Quote taken from Carla's responses to the Big Mom Group
questionnaire.

4. Hilary Price quote found at www.christianitytoday.com/outreach/
articles/introducingwoman.html.

5. Marcia Ford, www.marciaford.com/faqs.html.

6. Merriam-Webster's Online Dictionary, www.merriam-webster.com/dictionary/empower.

7. Carla Barnhill, "Competitive Balancing," Gifted for Leadership blog, http://blog.christianitytoday.com/giftedforleadership/2008/03/competitive_balancing.html.

8. Margaret Mead, quoted in Lynne Hybels, *Nice Girls Don't Change the World* (South Barrington, IL: Willow Creek Resources, 2005), 88, http://womenshistory.about.com/cs/quotes/a/qu_margaret mead.htm.

9. Hybels, *Nice Girls Don't Change the World,* 88.

Drop Me a Line!

Now that you've heard plenty from me, I'd love to hear from you! E-mail me with your stories, your reactions, your ideas, your questions, your complaints, or whatever at **caryn@carynrivadeneira.com.**

While you're at it, please visit me at **www.carynrivadeneira.com.** You can join the discussion on the blog, check out other things I've written, and see if I'm speaking in your neck of the woods.

Speaking of *speaking,* e-mail me at caryn@carynrivadeneira.com if you're interested in having me:

- speak at your women's or moms' group (or men's, dads', or mixed group for that matter!)
- speak or lead a workshop at your conference
- chat at or help facilitate your retreat

Before we say good-bye, a couple other quick—yet cool—things:

1. Visit ChristianBibleStudies.com. for a *free* Bible study based on this book. Just search for "When You Feel like Mama's Got a Fake I.D." Or visit www.carynrivadeneira.com and follow the links. It's *perfect* for your book club, women's group, or Bible study.

2. That friend you heard mentioned throughout this book, Carla Barnhill, and I have started a Revolution. The Mommy Revolution, that is. Check out what we're up to at www.themommy revolution.wordpress.com.

3. The Gifted for Leadership blog gave me an outlet to first write about moms and our identities. It's been sparking *needed* conversations ever since. Be sure to visit me—and a zillion other incredible voices—there at www.GiftedforLeadership.com.

Hope to hear from you soon. Blessings!

About the Author

Caryn Dahlstrand Rivadeneira is the mom of the three greatest kids ever created, the wife of a good, good man (not so hard to find after all!), and the writer and editor of, well, words and sentences. Though none of this keeps her from being equally that woman on the verge of losing her ever-loving mind as she tries to figure out a way to integrate her roles and responsibilities as mom to those best-ever kids, wife of that good man, and writer and editor of those sentences and all the trouble they cause.

She thanks God for the gifts in her life and opportunities she's had to edit *Marriage Partnership* and *Christian Parenting Today* magazine as well as the Gifted for Leadership blog. She can't believe she gets to write a mom column for *Today's Christian Woman* magazine and feels down-right blessed to be able to write for and speak to the wonderfully gifted and diverse women who make up the body of Christ. This is not to say she doesn't wish a little more sleep and "me-time" with these gifts and opportunities.

In her spare time, Caryn loves to read and go for walks. Her favorite state is Wisconsin, followed by Vermont, because it reminds her so much of Wisconsin. She graduated from Calvin College in Grand Rapids, Michigan, a place she also happens to love, though it doesn't remind her of Wisconsin. She lives in the western suburbs of Chicago with her husband, three kids, a bunny, three goldfish, and a huge snarly Rottweiler who lives on the flesh of intruders (as well as three cups a day of Wellness-brand dog food).

So you might want to call before popping by.